SECRETS OF SUPER SUCCESS

Subhash Lakhotia
Tax & Investment Consultant
Tax Guru: CNBC Awaaz

DIAMOND BOOKS

Publisher : **Diamond Pocket Books (P) Ltd.**
X-30, Okhla Industrial Area, Phase-II
New Delhi-110020
Phone : 011-40712200
E-mail : wecare@diamondbooks.in
Website : www.diamondbooks.in
Edition : 2025

Secrets of Super Success
By : Subhash Lakhotia

KNOW THE AUTHOR
Mr. Subhash Lakhotia

Mr. Subhash Lakhotia is the Director of R.N. Lakhotia & Associates LLP. He is an Income-tax practitioner for the last 40 years. He regularly writes in various national dailies. He is the Director of Lakhotia College of Taxation & Management. He is practicing as a consultant on tax planning, tax documentation and investment planning. He has also addressed a number of seminars and lectures on taxation and tax planning and is conducting the popular course known as 'Zero to Hero in Direct Taxes!'

He was selected as the best youth of India by the Lions International to represent India at the World Youth Congress held at Atlantic City, USA in 1970. He is Secretary General of Investors Club and President of Spiritual Club International and Unite to Invest (UTI). He is Chief Strategist of Real Estate Strategy Group and is actively associated with various professional bodies connected with real estate. He has written books on Income-tax, Investment, Real Estate and Spirituality. He is actively associated with Lions Clubs International. He has been awarded the "*Sahityashree*" award and *'The Suryadatta National Award, 2010"*. He is in the Governing Council of Proton Business School.

Mr. Subhash Lakhotia is conducting a very popular show "Tax Guru" on every Wednesday, Saturday and Sunday on 'CNBC AWAAZ', a popular TV Channel from the house of CNBC. Recently the 250th episode of Tax Guru was aired on the TV Channel. The National Television Awards, 2010 for *"Best Business Talk Show of the Year"* has been awarded to the Tax Guru programme.

Mailing Address:
Mr. Subhash Lakhotia
Tax & Investment Consultant
S-228, Greater Kailash-II,
New Delhi – 110048.
Phone: 011-29215434, 29215420,
Ph. 9810001665
Email: slakhotia@satyam.net.in
and thelakhotia@gmail.com

Preface

I have great pleasure in presenting this book for the benefit of all those persons who are interested to achieve Super Success in life.

Men and women, young and old all would find in this book practical secrets for super success in life.

I remember that Mark Twain once said that all you need in life is ignorance and confidence, the success is sure. But in today's context I feel that one should aim to achieve not just success but "Super Success" and this can become a reality if the reader were to read and adopt the mantras contained in this book for his super success. A successful man is he who received a great deal more from his fellow men, usually incomparably more than corresponds to his service to them, said Albert Einstein. Now the new generation, young and old, would surely benefit a lot from this book and I would feel my efforts rewarded if my readers derive super success in their life by reading this book.

I am thankful to my friend Shri Narendra Kumar Verma, the publisher of the book for taking all the pains to publish this book in such a short time.

August, 2010

Subhash Lakhotia

"Lakhotia Niwas"
S-228, Greater Kailash-II,
New Delhi – 110048.
Ph. 9810001665, 011-29215434
slakhotia@satyam.net.in

Contents

1

Yes, I want to be super successful

To all readers of this book I would like to give a guarantee that yes, you can be super successful in your life but only if you really want to be. Hence, the first point which requires a big *yes* from the readers is that you are, yes you are interested to become a super successful person. You want to dream about achieving super success in your life, this book will make it happen in reality for you. But please do remember the first important point which again and again I would like to emphasise is yes you really want to be. What all is written in this book coupled with your strong determination and finally the sunshine of the Almighty God will make you definitely a super successful person. Believe in this dictum. Have faith in this dictum and then proceed to read the subsequent pages of the book and finally when you end up the book, you find that yes your life is now making you super successful person in different walks of your life. Have faith in you, the power of faith is really great. It is amazing and it is really a magic of earth. Hence, do have the faith and do have the inclination to achieve super success in every walk of life. Think yourself. Yes you are the real super successful person. Think again and again and again and let your thinking itself turn out to make your road for achieving super success in your life. Never think you are weak, if you think that yes you are weak, then definitely weak you will be. Always think yourself strong. But the fact is you are really not strong. Then try to develop the qualities that will make you strong in different walks of life. But end of the day the answer is you have to think that yes I am not weak at all. I am strong and I am the real super successful person.

When I turn to last 60 years of my life, I find that yes I am very lucky to be a super successful person and I want to tell all my readers that analyse life span of your life till today. Screen it. Derive happiness from your past. Think of a brilliant future. Think that you are really a super successful person and if you are not, then you have to become and you will become. That would be the agenda in your mind. If you keep this single agenda in mind and let it be the goal of your life, then surely nothing can come in between to take your qualities of being a super successful person. Let me share with you some of my own experience of living my life till now. When I was young, a college student, a young lad of 20 years, at that time there was a competition by the Lions Club International and this competition was from whole of India, Burma and Nepal and the purpose of this competition was to select the best youth from whole of India, Burma and Nepal to take part in World Youth Congress in Atlantic City, USA. I did not have a wonderful background of studying in English medium high standard schools. But still I thought that one person has to be selected to attend the World Youth Congress in USA, then why not me. At present, when I look to the past, I find 40 years ago it was my self determination and my desire to participate in the contest and ultimately with the grace of the God I was selected as the best youth of India and was sent to Lions Club International Conference known as World Youth Congress held in Atlantic City way back in the year 1970. While the selection was in process for selecting the best youth of India, at times I was confused, at times I was perplexed, at times I was nervous and I thought that how I would be able to compete with dynamic youth coming from South India and the modern youth coming from Mumbai. However, with strong faith and determination, I made it possible. Finally in June 1970 I flew from Kolkata straight to USA and that was my first trip by aircraft and that too not in India but straight from India to USA. I was not even aware how to tie the seat belt while I sit in the aircraft. It was my first experience to travel abroad and that too alone. Believe me again when I say that at any point of time in your life if you find that new opportunity rocks your door, try to think fast and try to grab the opportunity and work hard and work hard with a bigger goal, then surely you are going to have a super success in your life. Similarly, 5 years ago it was 9 o'clock in the morning while I was having my breakfast and watching the TV show on one of the Business Channel known as Morning Breakfast Show. This was a show by some foreigner giving tips about investments etc. Very rarely it happens that I watch TV while having my breakfast. But that day it so happened that I spent almost half an hour watching the entire TV show conducted by one of the topmost TV personalities of the world. After I had seen the TV show I found the TV show giving tips and guidance of investment was pretty good. But in half an hour time lot of time was spent on matters connected with investment and divorce, investment and credit card, investment and house loan etc., etc. The show was good as it was giving lot of knowledge and information. But personally I felt the show was not so good from the point of view of the investors in India specially looking to life style as also the investment pattern and other cultural matters of India's population. I then thought that I should give my views to the Editor of the T.V. Channel. I then sent a letter to the Editor of the TV Channel saying that the TV show on investment was not so good and what is needed is something different for the Indian viewers. I am happy to inform my readers that my idea got attention of the Editor of a leading TV Channel and finally arrived a love letter for me to present and host a special TV Show on CNBC Awaaz and thereafter I started presenting the TV show known as Tax

Guru on the said CNBC Awaaz Channel. Just for the purpose of inspiring the readers of my book I am happy to inform that this year the National Television Awards 2010 were announced recently and my TV Show Tax Guru was awarded the Best Business Talk Show of the year. Anyway the credit of this goes only to my viewers who have expressed their love and affection to my TV Show. But the fact remains that it was determination and something new I had thought of and I had tried to implement my thinking by taking an opportunity to write to the Editor without knowing him and without any hesitation and finally the Editor accepted my view point but thereafter I tried to put in the best in me and finally came the TV Show Tax Guru. Dear Readers, Believe me when I say that you in your own sphere of life, in your own activity whether in business or profession or whether it is studies or in any other walk of life, you can achieve super success by taking advantage of the secrets of super success mentioned in this book but please do remember that it is your dedication and keen desire to achieve super success that alone would be instrumental in bringing super success at your door step. Similarly when I see my past, I find that nearly 30 years ago I had thought of setting up new innovative Educational Programme on Income-tax to be called "Zero to Hero in Income-tax" and let me tell you that this course made roars in whole of India and way back 30 years ago The Telegraph newspaper in Kolkata published a special story about this innovative course conducted by me. Well the purpose of writing some of the facts about my life is just to inspire the readers of the book that one should always sit down and think of the past achievements and aim at achieving new vistas in life relating to success in the coming years. But finally do have faith that your keen desire and strong determination towards your desired goal would make you a super successful jewel in your field.

2

Landmark decisions may bring super success to you

Whenever a point comes for taking important decisions, please screen all the aspects very carefully and only thereafter take a final call on the subject matter. Please do remember that any landmark decision taken by you may be the road to your prosperity and may be the road to bring super success to you in your life. Hence, one of the important secrets of super success is to respect the landmark decision and at any point of time whenever occasion arises to take such an important landmark decision, but surely think calmly coolly and thereafter only take the landmark decision in your life. I remember my father Shri R.N. Lakhotia who was a Class one Income-tax Officer took a landmark decision way back in the year 1962 to resign from the Income-tax Department and to start his own career in profession. It was definitely a very difficult management decision to think of leaving a lucrative government job but still he left it and thereafter was on his own. After leaving the government job he started writing large number of books on Income-tax, conducting seminars and this landmark decision which was taken by him in coordination, consultation and inspiration also of my mother late Shrimati Asha Rani Lakhotia made my father see wonderful vistas of happy and super successful life just as a result of this single management decision which he had taken way back in the year 1962. However, do please remember that whenever occasion or opportunity arises to take a management decision, at that point of time screen all the plus and the minus aspects of the decision to be taken. But once you have taken the decision, then do not go in back gear. My father has written over 500 books on income-tax which happens to be the largest number of books written by any author in the whole of the world. He is also regarded as a well-known author of income-tax in India. My father tells me that he has also seen a time when he had written his first book on income-tax and he went door to door of various publishers and requested him to publish his book. But no one was interested to publish the book of a person who was not known. It was at that point of time when a landmark decision was taken by him and again it was a joint decision by my father and my mother to start a publishing house of our own and thereafter the publishing house known as Asha Publishing House was born in our family. Just imagine if my father would have been sitting quiet with a gloomy face because no publisher was ready to publish his book, then today so many hundreds of books written by him would not have seen the light of the day. He had no experience in the publishing line. At that time he was himself a young lad of just 28 years. But the landmark decision taken by him led him to write books, start publishing house and live a super successful life. Later on I joined our family's Publishing House in the year 1965. In whatever field you want to achieve super success, you definitely can achieve it but just write down what super success you want. In which field you want super success and let innovation and let hard work be the driving force to achieve your super success. At any cost you have to achieve super success in your life , just stick to a single focused agenda and you will surely fulfil this desire with flying colours.

3

Don't ponder over other's success, just see your road map

If you want to become a super successful person, then one of the important secrets of becoming a super successful person is do not ponder over others activities in the development and the growth. Just continue to see and watch your own road map leading to the road of super success in your life. It is just wastage of time, talent and energy in pondering over the success stories of others including your friends, relatives and others whom you meet in different walks of life. Just aim at a single point to care and think of making your presence in a big manner. Just think that you have to become the real super successful hero whose life has to be emulated by others. Think this, think and think again because most of the people forget the road to their super success just because they are interested in trying analyzing and developing jealousy due to the growth and success of others. Hence, to achiève your super success do not ever think about the prosperity and progress of others but only aim at making your life line of progress always moving in the right direction and move up and up and also not stopping till you have reached your target of being a real super successful person. Don't think it to be a dream but let it be your mission statement which has to be achieved by you.

4

Jot down 12 qualities of super successful person and start implementing them month wise

Just jot down a list of at least 12 important qualities which you want to achieve to become a super successful person. Write down on a piece of paper these 12 qualities of head and heart and try to devote a month for each quality. Try to think that you have to achieve one quality a month and just in one year when you are able to achieve 12 qualities, then surely you become one of the super stars to be known as a super successful person. Let these 12 qualities of a super successful personality be imbibed by you and try your level best to achieve a successful winning over these 12 qualities and do believe me when I say that if you demarcate a time limit of one month for development of one quality then at the end of the year you find that in 12 months you have developed 12 important qualities in life, then definitely it is going to be a wonderful time for you to become a super successful person in your life. Just give this theme a try and experience for yourself the road for your own self which is going to make you a real super successful person.

5

High Self-esteem

Do maintain self esteem always high. I remember E.G. White who said that the Lord is disappointed when people place a low estimate upon themselves. He desires His chosen heritage to value themselves according to the price He has placed upon them. Gŏd wanted them, else He would not have sent His Son on such an expensive errand to redeem them. He has a use for them, and He is well pleased when they make very high demands upon Him, that they may glorify His name. They may expect large things if they have faith in His promises.

Hence, always keep a high self esteem of yourself and never ever fear unnecessarily. Super successful persons never fear in life. They are not afraid of any problem in life and if they are not having fear in their life, they are able to make progress in life and achieve the target of being a super successful person. Sometimes those in business may get a fear about the future of their business, about the future export order, may be about the cancellation of the order and fear may also be there about the rejection of the goods produced in the factory. Another person may fear about labour trouble in the factory leading to closure of the factory and ultimately a big loss in the factory, someone may fear what happens if I fall sick on the day of exam and I will not be able to pass the exams, unnecessarily do not ever let fear come near you. Your personality will be shackled if you are near the fear bowl. Hence, do not fear unnecessarily. If at all you are to fear in life, then just fear the Almighty God alone and other than Him do not fear anyone.

6

Never ever compromise on your Basic Belief for achieving Super Success

One of the key points for achieving super success is that one should never compromise on the basic belief which he is having. However, one can always have a re-look in forming that belief. But once the beliefs are strong, then one should always adhere to those beliefs and should not compromise on them. This type of thinking on the one hand makes you strong and makes you adhere to your own goals which have to be achieved by your belief.

One such example of a person who has already achieved super success and has great faith in his beliefs relates to one Indian born billionaire Pankaj Oswal and his wife Radhika Oswal. This couple is very rich and presently based in Australia. Now they are constructing their very posh residential mansion in Perth. Being of Indian origin and although based in Australia, Pankaj and Radhika have very strong belief of being vegetarian all the time and simultaneously promoting vegetarianism through innovative ideas. Recently the work was in progress in their new massive mansion which is located in the exclusive suburb of Peppermint Grove and which is likely to be finished sometime in the year 2011. This construction activity for his residential house is named as The Taj-on-Swan Mansion and is being constructed on one of the most expensive piece of land in Australia. Now this NRI owner of this prestigious mansion has put a ban on the construction site for consumption of meat by the working staff. Although the construction, forestry, mining and engineering union of Australia has criticized the ban of not consuming meat on the construction site but still Pankaj and Radhika are defending the meat ban saying, "It is our home and it is destroying us environmentally, economically and socially". To be a vegetarian or not to be a vegetarian is a personal choice of the reader but the theme which I would like to emphasize is that for achieving super success let your basic belief prevail all along in life. In this case of Pankaj and Radhika Oswal they are constructing one of the most beautiful houses on the earth in Australia which will have a very big swimming pool which would be more than ten times bigger than the average backyard of an Australian house owner. But the fundamental theme which I would like to emphasize upon is that develop your own beliefs, perceptions and liking and never compromise on those beliefs in particular. This adherence to non-compromising belief will make you really super successful person in the years to come. However, one can always have a re-look at the beliefs so that they do not come in your midway to stop your super success race in different walks of life.

7

Follow the idea of 'Mitch' Scooter from Japan

The super successful person always thinks of doing things somewhat in a different fashion. The theme of doing somewhat differently from other persons makes a person shine in his vision, shine in his strategy because a super successful person always at every point of time thinks of doing somewhat innovative style in presentation, in get up, in every sphere, in every way, in every walk of life. The classic example of this theme is from Kimco Scooter Manufacturing Company based in Japan. Shortly in Tokyo, the Tokyo Motor Cycle Show 2010 would be launched. In this Motor Cycle Show more than one hundred companies from different parts of the world would be participating and would be showcasing their products concerning the scooter. It will definitely be a difficult task to draw the attention of the visitors. Hence, Kimco Company of Japan has thought of really innovative style to draw the attention of the audience attending the great big Motor Cycle Show. Now the 'Mitch' Scooter which comes from the House of Kimco of Japan is embedded with 100000 Swarovski Crystals. It is a well known fact that the Swarovski Crystal today are world famous and are known to be superb in the world. Hence, just imagine when this scooter from the House of Kimco Company is being displayed in the show of forthcoming Motor Cycle Show 2010, then surely all those persons attending the said show will be tempted to see this scooter with a rare 100000 Swarovski Crystals affixed on the scooter itself. We are not going to participate and attend the Tokyo Motor Cycle Show of 2010. But definitely by closing your eye you can visualize how wonderful and great this scooter would be looking when 100000 Swarovski Crystals are embedded upon this scooter. Although Kimco Company of Japan may not be able to compete with the goodwill of Honda or Yamaha Models but surely it is going to draw a great bit attention of all those who are going to attend the Tokyo Motorcycle Show 2010. This unique and innovative idea of decorating the scooter which is participating in the Motorcycle Show 2010 is surely an innovative idea to achieve super success in the Trade Show or Exhibition. One can get a real inspiring idea from the innovative idea proposed to be implemented by Kimco Company of Japan to decorate its scooter with 100000 Swarovski Crystals. The moral of this example is that if you are thinking of achieving super success at any business event etc. and more particularly in the forthcoming exhibition which you might like to participate in for your products or services, then surely do something innovative to attract the attention of the crowd participating in the exhibition or the event which will definitely make you achieve super success in your activity which you are dilating.

8

Meditate and think Unique Idea in your business activity for your Super Success

In business or profession, super success does not come instantly. But in the existing crowd of businessmen as also existing crowd of professional persons if you are interested to make your mark and your presence, then it is now the time for you to think some unique idea and make that idea your source of achieving super success. Question now arises as to how to think of unique idea to be implemented in your business. Well the simple answer is to rise early in the morning, meditate and think and just think and think alone. Jot down any innovative idea which comes in your mind. Not one not two but ten, twenty or hundred ideas may come, let it come. All you have to do is just to write down the innovative new ideas which might come in your mind on one fine morning. Once you have finished with writing down all that comes in your mind, now is the time to mediate on each single idea which you might have thought about. Examine the idea, screen it, judge yourself the strong points in favour of that particular idea, so also think about the weaknesses of that idea and finally if you find that the weak points outnumber the good features of your idea, then just lock it in the back of your drawer. Go on doing so for the next idea and the next idea. At the end of the day, you will find that you have been successful in finding one unique innovative idea for your business activity. Try to develop inner faith and confidence in your own idea. This faith and confidence can be achieved merely by meditating again and again and again on a single idea and screening in the mind the negatives and positives of that idea. Do remember when you want to be the super successful person in your business or professional activity, then surely something will have to be done in such a manner which is not being done in that type of business or profession by others.

Couple of months ago, one big real estate developer approached me and wanted me along with him to meditate on some new innovative business activity idea. Well I enjoy this type of thrilling activities which inspires me and which takes my creativity to new heights because as I meditate and as I think into the business activity of some another person, my mind starts jumping up and down and again down and up and then I find myself that I have come out with some of those real practical innovative and unique ideas which may look to be simple but might have lost track of by the person engaged in his business or profession. For example, to this real estate developer I gave the innovative idea that if he wants to sell luxury apartments with a fat price tag, then the answer is that let him offer one complimentary office space or showroom space or Mall space to all those persons who are interested to invest in the luxury apartments being constructed by him. Well different innovative ideas and thinking will emerge in your mind at that point of time when you just start meditating. However, before meditation the first important work to be done is to have faith in the theme that yes, if I think about some unique activity, only then I can start my business in a much more profitable way.

To inspire the readers of this book I would like to tell them about similar experience by Sonu Shivdasani who is a person of Indian origin but presently he is a Non-Resident Indian who can be complemented for running some of the most wonderful luxurious resorts you can ever find on this earth. Most of the Indians know very little about Sonu and this is mainly because of the reason that although Sonu is Indian, but he has spent most of his life abroad. That is the reason people know very little of this wonderful man. Initially Sonu was managing the Global Portfolio of the Family Businesses from Geneva to Lagos and London. But it appears that this work did not impress his inner world. He along with his Swedish wife Eva thought of starting something unique in the hotel industry. They thought of a little less place known as Maldives. Now they thought of starting a hotel in Maldives. It might sound somewhat crazy that a person with no background in the hotel industry was now thinking of starting a hotel and that too in a foreign country. Like any other hotelier he was making a bid and the auction to build a hotel in Maldives but was not successful in getting the bid accepted. Finally Sonu did not stop and he went on to take on lease the island and then to start a hotel thereon. Our readers would agree that it is definitely a tough time to start pouring money in that business activity which is not known to you. Just like a foreign country a foreign business the ABCD of which is not known to you and then you invest substantial money in that, definitely is a very risky business proposal. But it did not bring any risk in the minds of Sonu and he started developing luxurious resorts initially at Maldives and later on to more than twenty destinations all over the world. Recently a cover story about Sonu was written by Vir Singh Sanghvi in the Sunday Magazine Brunch (Hindustan Times). A glance at the photographs printed with the cover story makes you interesting to visit these luxurious resorts run by Sonu Shivdasani. I could see from the photographs that all the resorts which he has built are par excellent. They are not at all routine in nature and they reflect something excellent relaxation and enjoyment places in the world. Well this type of success achieved by Sonu has made him a super successful person in the luxury resorts. The main reason was only of some unique ideas and thoughts which were ultimately implemented by Sonu. "Sonu", as Vir Sanghvi quotes, "has the philosophy that works because it has turned many conventional conceptions of luxury on their head". It is the intelligent thinking by making something unique for your business or profession that will take you in the wonderland of a super successful person.

Similarly, the young 26 year old Hari Shanker Narayanan was crazy right from his childhood about computer games. He studied Mechanical Engineering. Right from the beginning he learnt computer programming side by side and spent most of his time writing codes for computer engineering students. He enjoyed this activity. Hari Shanker was a notorious and mischievous kid in his school. But Hari Shankar considers this quality as an essential characteristic for a game developer. Right from day one Hari Shanker has been thinking about unique innovative ideas for his business activity and that is the reason right now Hari Shanker is currently working on an action – Adventure – SCI – FI title, again a new computer game which is expected to bring laurels to him. Equally interesting is the story of Abhijit Jaipal who was doing his summer internship with Motorola at their Headquarters in Illinois sometime in the year 2000. At that time he realized the tremendous potential of the mobile media and Synquafyak was founded by him in May 2008. He works very hard about 16 to 18 hours a day and the real money and the real super successful person he will be because of thinking about new ideas for mobile application. A large number of young boys and girls are there working in different parts of the world as a part of mobile application developer who have the world at their finger tips and these young creative and successful persons are all telling the single story which has brought them super success and the story is with reference to some unique idea first to be thought of and then ultimately to be implemented. Equally interesting is the story of Rohit Singhal who started as a radiologist and ultimately began his story by setting up a workstation with three people in a garage. Now in last three years his company has developed over 70 mobile applications for the Apple, Facebook and others. The real life story of Rohit Singhal would be inspiring to a large number of our readers specially when a radiologist is turned into a mobile application developer and he has proved that it is possible for everyone including you to develop something new, something innovative but only when you think about innovative ideas and vistas.

To think of something unique idea and that to implement such ideas calls for very hard work. I remember when Hrithik Roshan, the famous hero in the Bollywood made his debut as a singer in his latest film *Kites*. He sang a song in this film but he had to rehearse a lot. From early in the morning he had to start with *sa re ga ma* with hand movement trying to reach the highest scale and finally he has been able to make it. Do remember that if you want to be super successful person, then at least you have to think something unique and then implement that with hard work and finally you will find that super success is achieved.

Recently the Exchange Bar and Grill, which is in the bustling shock and pub of Grammercy Park, New York has thought of some new innovative idea based on the concept of the Stock Exchange. In this restaurant the menu prices will reflect Live Stock. What would be the value of the pint of beer? Let the market decide where the prices for food and the beverages will fluctuate like the Stock Exchange according to the demand of the item. This type of innovative idea has really brought super success to this restaurant in Manhattan. Similarly is also going to be the story of Stemcell. Stemcell is a new concept the world over. In India also many companies have started the business activity of Stemcell Processing Laboratories and preserving the Stemcell. Doing this type of activity would result into super success because these activities have been done in somewhat unique style and idea.

9

Robust Health: Your Priority No. 1 just for your Super Success

Long time back when I was young going to school even at that time I have been hearing that 'health is wealth'. In the initial journey in my life I did not have much faith of this dictum, in spite of the fact that this dictum was narrated even to you by one and all be it relatives or the elders or family members or your teachers. But as I passed some more years in my life I realised that for your super success the formula number one is definitely your robust health. Just imagine if you are not healthy, what you will do to achieve super success. If you are not healthy, how will you put in your best 24 X 7 for achieving the super success in the field in which you want to achieve? Just think if you are down with illness on your back and locked in the room of a hospital, how will you ever dream of having a super success. Money you may have. Money can buy many new ideas and many new projects. Money can also buy new ventures and money can become profitable tool for you. Money can multiply your money. But the fact is that if you do not have a robust health, what will you do to control your money? How will you control your money and enjoy your money? Well for the benefit of my readers, I would like to emphasize very strongly that it is just your robust health which will find place in your agenda book for achieving super success in any walk of your life and believe me when I say that I have watched very closely the movements of famous and rich and top people. One common thing for all of them is that it is their robust health which has been responsible for making their debut in achieving super success in their field.

Most of my readers would also have received the sermon from their elders and the family members as also the well wishers that 'health is wealth'. The big dictum still has not been able to pinpoint your ears so strong that you start caring about your health from day one. Anyway forget the past. Forget what has happened. Forget about your good and bad health in the past. Just think today. Think today, think for tomorrow and think about achieving robust health for whole of your life. It is true that merely thinking about robust health will not make us achieve robust health. What then we do? Well, the answer is to start your journey to make yourself a personality with robust health, a personality bubbling with enthusiasm, a personality which is cheerful always, a personality always for marching ahead and all this will become a reality only when you find that you are a person possessing robust health. When you think that you have to go again and again to my doctor for headache, for migraine, for blood pressure, you feel shy. Don't be shy in the presence of the family members or relatives or friends but you would surely feel shy, you would feel unhappy while you are alone in the room. Just think and just meditate that robust health you are to achieve and then start your action plan for achieving your robust health. Well, for most of the readers it is just the following general principles that will make you achieve your robust health. The first important principle is to have the greatest faith in the fact that it is my health which is number one in the development of my personality. Do have great faith in the dictum that 'health is wealth'. If you do not have that much faith right now, then it is worthwhile chanting this mantra in the morning and similar chanting of the health mantra in the day time and finally closing your day by chanting the health mantra while you go to your bed. The constant chanting of the mantra "health is wealth" will surely imbibe in your mind and you will foresee the advantages of maintaining a robust health. Do think that unless there is a health, you will not be able to achieve anything in your life. You can do many things of the world. You can buy the luxuries of the world. But definitely you cannot buy your health and happiness. Happiness also plays a vital role in your super success. Do remember that only when you are in a robust health, you will become happy. Hence, to ensure that you maintain robust health, it is time right now to make this health maintenance programme the number one top programme in your agenda which alone will make it possible to make you a super successful personality in the years to come.

Maintaining good health rests on time tested fundamental principles which have not changed in the last hundred thousand years. I am of the view that basic fundamental principles will not change even in the next thousand years to come. What all is needed is to start your day with normal life schedule of 30/45 minutes morning walk coupled with some light exercises or yoga. Well, like most of the people if you find that you are not able to carry out your regular dose of routine exercises, then surely you have the option now to visit gym. Take extensive advantage of gym or the health equipments installed in your house. Anyway, the ultimate object is to ensure that your health is perfect which is possible only by carrying out your daily routine of exercise and morning walk. The importance of health also depends upon your positive and negative thoughts coming in your mind. Thoughts of different types and varieties definitely will be coming to your mind again and again but the super successful person always tries to see that he does not let negative thoughts monitor his personality. Do away with negative thoughts instantly and just think on the positive thoughts. Your thinking about the positive thoughts will bring for you positive rays of hope for your personality development and ultimately will be responsible for your super success. The next simple point with regard to the maintenance of the robust health lies in maintaining a disciplined life style of food intake. Keep your timing almost fixed for your breakfast, for your lunch as well as for your dinner. This simple activity alone will be responsible to make you in good shape for your wonderful health. The food you take also plays a very very vital role in making you healthy. Whether you take vegetarian food or a non-vegetarian food is definitely your personal choice. However, from my experience I can say that if you are a vegetarian by choice in taking your food, then surely you will be able to maintain a better health in the years to come. More particularly those who want to achieve super success and all those who would like to work more fast and also for long years should depend mainly on vegetarian food and more specifically on fresh fruits and fresh vegetables coupled with small dose of dry fruits.

I recollect the actual incident which took place about five years ago. A client of mine came to my office at about 11 A.M. in the morning. We were to leave for a business meeting with one young, smart entrepreneur who had lot of business ideas, he was actually a genius but was without money. My client definitely was not genius but he was a money genius i.e. he had a lot of money. I thought if the marriage takes place of my client with this young genius person with no money, then both of them can make a lasting marriage and both of them can benefit. The time was fixed for 11 A.M. in the morning. My client arrives half an hour late. I asked him what was the reason and the simple answer was his high blood pressure. From his face my client looked little tired, not very enthusiastic, little bit depressed too. When I found that he was not comfortable in attending the business meeting, because of the blood pressure problem, I asked him to better check his blood pressure. The blood pressure equipment from my residence was brought in and his blood pressure revealed fantastic very high blood pressure which according to the doctor required instant and immediate admission to a hospital. Surely for a businessman always first is business. My friend also believed in this concept always but what to do for ill health. Firstly, the meeting had to be cancelled. My friend was rushed to the hospital and he was admitted because of his extreme high blood pressure. Then he returned back home. He had telephoned me again two days later to fix up the timing for a business meeting with the young entrepreneur with no money but with the ideas and I told my friend that last week we had an appointment with the young entrepreneur but due to your bad health you were hospitalized and that the meeting now cannot take place because after the cancellation of our meeting; the young entrepreneur had already tied up with another industrialist and financer and has concluded the deal. This is a real life story which took place five years ago. Now when I met that young entrepreneur who had no money five years ago but had ideas and had vision and had some important innovative applications and strategies in his mind, he is a man now worth Rs.50 crores and this was possible only because of marriage between some other angel financier who had left his money with this young entrepreneur and the story continued of their growth year after year. Well, the moral of this story is that if you are not giving proper care to your health, it is possible that you may at one point of time in your life miss out one of the biggest opportunities of your life to make you super success in your field. Hence, always care and care for your health and keep health as the number one agenda on your list.

When we talk about health, please also do remember that it is not that we have to keep on talking about health and health and health at every hour of the day. What however is needed is just to note that health should be always taken as number one priority item which should become a part of your daily routine. Hence, let health maintenance and health upkeep be your routine agenda just like we eat and sleep every day. In the same manner, we should carry out all the activities concerning our health in the routine manner so that our bad health does not become at any point of time a constraint in our personality development for achieving super success in our life.

To conclude, if you want to be a super success achiever in your life then do start taking full care for your health. Let morning walk, yoga as also exercise be a part of your daily routine agenda. Let the thousand year old dictum namely – "Health is Wealth" be a part of the wonderful mantra on which you might like to be embedded with a focused objective of becoming a real super success achiever. Also do remember that only when you are healthy, you are able to inspire your colleagues as well as those persons who come in your contact in different walks of life. Believe in the above dictum, implement it and so the path of super success is at your door steps only.

10

Determination : an important agenda for your Super Success

To my dear young friends, I mean the young boys and girls right now studying in school, the single focused agenda on their mind screen should be determination and determination only. It is this one word – "Determination" which can change their entire life cycle. The young boys and girls of the present day India have great challenges as well as opportunities in years to come. But all challenges can be faced without any problem but only if they are addicted to the theme of "determination". For young and old the theme of determination would act as a key note pointer for a prosperous and bright future. I am personally a great follower of one famous dictum of Walt Disney, the person who had founded the Disneyland. It was Walt Disney who always used to say that - "If you can Dream it, you can do it". I think the present day young school going friends of mine would, in particular, take inspiration from this theme and start dreaming of passing out with flying colours and by securing a real good rank in the class.

My friend, Dr. Piyush Kumar, a publisher by profession recently told me about actual life story of a young girl from Chennai. This girl had lost both her arms in one accident. In spite of this mishap, she was determined to secure a very good result in her board exams. Finally, she has secured over 98% marks and the single fact responsible for her to achieve this was her determination which made her fight against all adversities. This young girl also had the pleasure of meeting Dr. Abdul Kalam, the former President of India. Now the girl is in New Delhi in Hindu College. She is very popular in the College and she is ever smiling. Her desire is to become a U.N. Coordinator. I am sure that she would achieve it because she has a great determination. Also please do remember the dictum of India's greatest son – Swami Vivekananda who always used to say – "Never think you are weak". Please emulate this great saying of Vivekananda to reap the fruits of success in life.

When I was young, just twenty years of age at that time in the year 1970, the Lions International had organised an all India competition of selecting the best youth of India to participate in the World Youth Congress which was held in Atlantic City, USA. I had read about it. I thought let me make a try. At that time I had passed out from a Hindi medium school. But with determination as well as with the grace of God I had the proud pleasure of being selected as the best youth of India and then I spent a month in U.S.A., U.K. and was just thrilled with my tour. Please do remember that your keen determination can do wonders in your student life and also in later life. Likewise, I remember that I had the desire to win a silver cup in "English Debate" in the school. At that time my English was not that strong but hard determination made it happen for me and I won the first prize in Class 9th English Debate.

Another small little advice which I would like to give to young friends is to take care of time. The lost time is never found again. It was Benjamin Franklin who said that "Lost time is never found again and what we call time enough, always proves little enough". So save time, use it in best possible way. Time should not be wasted so also the money should not be wasted. Habit of saving money and not wasting it should start when you are young. It was Benjamin Franklin who said that "Don't give me too much for the whistle". In today's context use everything but do not just waste be it time or money.

Another small little point which I would like to share with my young friends is that at your next Birthday party do take out a slice of Birthday Cake for a road side poor boy who just cannot afford to buy this piece of cake. If you do this small act of charity then when you eat your slice of Birthday cake you would feel as if it is "Food from Heaven". Also do not forget to say prayers before you retire for a good night sleep and next day morning do offer salutations to your parents. Everyday, make it a part of your life. I wish good luck to every reader and would request you to write to me your thoughts and feelings on my small little thoughts. You can e-mail to me at slakhotia@satyam.net.in.

Every day we come across new innovative and unique ideas connected with business activity which is responsible for your super success in your respective business activity. If however, you do not have any business activity of your own and you are interested to start some new business activity, then also it is time for you to meditate and think about some new business activity. Merely sitting down with folded hand cannot give you super success in trade and industry. If you want to achieve super success, you cannot afford to sit down with folded hands even on a single day. I recollect the actual life story of a young IIT student. He is a young man of 22 and is a final year student of Masters in Mathematics and Computing. He thought of innovative business idea which has made his new business a super success. His new initiative known as Phokat copy provides completely free photocopy services to college goers. Well, one can think and meditate how it is possible to provide free photocopy service to the students. Someone may think that it may be a purely social service idea. But the fact remains that for this young man it is ingenious business model whereby applying his unique idea he is able to provide free photocopy services to college going students. To end this suspense his great idea is that he provides free photocopy services to the students and subsiding it with advertisement on the back side of the page. This is a new venture started just six months ago in Delhi and it has been initial success because nearly four lakh sheets have been supplied across different college students of Delhi and now this young entrepreneur is thinking to take the same model in different parts of India. Thus, always think of super and unique business idea which alone will make your success story in the years to come.

Never think that to start your business activity you need always a big infrastructure. Generally the youth in particular think that unless you have sufficient money power to start your big business venture, you cannot make it a success. This is absolutely wrong and incorrect dictum. Just see the history of Pilgate and Steve Jobs who has started the career in a garage shed and so also Michael Dell started out in a single room and still it was their unique ideas in business which have made them achieve success in a short time. Likewise the new iPad has clearly demonstrated that it can hold his own hand in the gaining market against the existing market leaders. Again the answer is your unique business idea making your super success come to your doorsteps. If you want to make your super success in business activity, then you can also take inspiration from Swami Pranavananda. He is a spiritual leader and a monk but who makes his living out of fashion. Today his G.F. Textiles Private Limited caters to around 20 Global Brands. You could see this spiritual Swami at the recently concluded International Fashion Trade Show and even participating in this Trade Show he was in his saffron dhoti and shawl. Likewise the new Medanta Medicity which has recently opened in Gurgaon is spread over 43 acres of land and is promoted by famous Cardiac Surgeon Dr. Naresh Trehan. In this new Medanta Medicity which is housed in 14 storeyed building and which has 1500 beds together with 45 operative theatres and a huge team of 1000 doctors. It is this type of innovative thinking and big ideas which has been responsible for making Medicity a unique destination for medical treatment. Also think of London based

Layfiel who is a British Serial Entrepreneur and he is with an abundance of business ideas and frustrated with lack of funds from regular banking sources and now he has tried a new noble business model. He is offering a 10 percent stake in himself for pound run million, thereby valuing himself at Pound 10 million. This 36 year old James Layfield who has to his credit three profitable businesses under his never ever limited banner. This practice unique idea came to him on his last buttering while he was cycling. Now due to this unique idea and unique offering Layfield has put on a table a 10 percent stake in himself which means that a prospective investor could get his take in any business he floats at a future point of time.

The unique idea in your business activity by Sandeep Maheshwari is also such that will inspire you to think of this theme for your super success in the business. A freelance photographer turned entrepreneur, Sandeep Maheshwari took the idea from the names of the Indian Advertising and Marketing Industry in respect of ready stock images. He came to the conclusion that commercial stock photography which won a US Dollar 1.5 billion industry globally was virtually absent in India and so he brought in imagesbazar.com in the year 2006 with just 14600 images. Right now over 8 lakh images are on this site thereby taking it the world's largest stock of images where one can search, purchase and download as per his need. In a short span of nearly four years over 6000 brands and more than 42 countries use images from his website. His example is just a wonderful inspiration to continue to strive for excellence for super success.

11

Develop the quality of Forgiveness

One of the special feature of a super successful person is that he always forgives. Do develop the virtue of forgiveness. The following words of Mother Teresa would anyway inspire you to forgive one and all:-

People are often unreasonable, illogical and self-centred; forgive them anyway. If you are kind, people will accuse you of selfish motives; be kind anyway. If you are successful, you will win some false friends and true enemies; succeed anyway.

If you are honest and frank, people may cheat you; be honest and frank anyway. What you spend yours building, someone could destroy overnight; build anyway. If you find serenity and happiness, they may be jealous; be happy anyway.

The good that you do today, people will often forget tomorrow, do good anyway.

Give the best you have and it may never be enough; give the wold the best you've got, anyway. In the final analysis, it is between you and God; it was never between you and them, anyway.

12

Your Kind Heart

A kind hearted person is a winner always. Hence, a super successful person must have a kind heart. Another big advantage of being a kind hearted person is that you command respect from one and all; hence, a super successful person must always be kind hearted. No cost but only gain if you are a kind hearted person. Hence, emulate the good principle of being a kind hearted person always.

13

Time to teach your children the basic qualities of Super Success

If you have achieved super success in your field and now proudly you can call yourself a real super successful person but I feel that the real super success of yours would be achieved when you are able to make your children also super successful. This is possible in a practical manner by teaching your children the basic qualities of super successful person.

Hence, even when your children are young, it is your duty to teach them the simple but important qualities of super success in life. Believe me when I say that the sermon given by you to your children will certainly help your children to get hold of these good qualities in their practical daily life. Hence, the qualities of hard work, honesty, integrity, ethics etc. should be told to your children so that while they are still young they learn these qualities which will go directly into their blood and make them super successful person. Do remember that your real super success lies in making your own children achieve to qualities of a super successful person.

14

If you want to win, you need an Action Plan

One of the world's topmost tennis player Nikolai Davydenko feels that there is no hopeless situation in the dictum that 'If you want to win, you need an action plan'. It may be recalled here that the 28 year Nikolai a really very talented sports person and equally he has the reputation of being a hard worker. He does not have any special physical advantage but still he has achieved remarkable results for which the credit goes to his incredible work ethics. Presently Nikolai lives in Germany, plays Tennis the world-over and in the year 2009 he won the ATT World Tour Final and in January 2010 he won the ATT World Tour in Doha. He strongly believes that if you want to win in life, you must have an action plan. Same is equally good for every person who wants to achieve super success in any field. For achieving super success and not just success it is time for you right now to have an action plan for yourself and then plan the action one by one.

Do remember that your action plan will be instrumental in taking you to new heights in the respective fields in which you want to win. Hence, it is time now for you to just think and write on a piece of paper the areas in which you want to win. The winner will be that guy who is a super successful person in that area. Super successful you would like to be. Well, you would be, but for that do prepare a detailed and meticulous action plan, review the plan again and again and then you see your road to super success coming nearer to you and to you alone.

15

Agenda at Night – Your road to Super Success

One of the greatest inventors of all time is Emerson. His name as one of the greatest inventors is accepted, recognized and respected the world over not today, not yesterday but will be respected and remembered in the years to come. This gentleman gave us electricity and similarly gave us small little hundreds of inventions which we are using today with success and for our benefit. The new generation will also continue to use his innovations in the years to come. One day, one person asked him as to what was the reason of his success. The plain and simple one line reply given by Emerson was that every night before he goes to bed, he prepares his agenda for the next day and then on the next day he sees the agenda and goes on working on the same. My dear readers, if you want to achieve super success in the field in which you want to, then it is the time to take a clue from the life style of Emerson that is to prepare your next day's agenda at night. I guarantee that if you make this habit as a part of your life, as a part of your routine habit, you will see that you are going to be a super successful person in any stream of life which is dear to you.

Please do remember that preparing your agenda for activity for the next day on the previous night really would push your focused attention to the management of the next day. By preparing this agenda for the next day you are able to concentrate your energy in a focused manner in all those activities written on a piece of paper with the heading *"Things for tomorrow"*. Your agenda helps you to save wastage of your time and energy because due to the next day's agenda by the time next day arrives you start the day with a bright sun light but before that you are ready with your focused mind knowing all that you have to do for the long day. In comparison with a person who prepares agenda at night and a person who does not prepare agenda and gets to his workplace the next day, couple of hours are just wasted in thinking what to do, which activity to take up for today, which not to take up, which is the priority one for the day, what is the forecast to be made urgently and then substantial portion of this energy goes wasted. Thus, for a super successful person the aim is of achieving the theme of conserving his energy and this is possible only if you plan to prepare your next day's agenda on the previous night. Your agenda at night preparation activity will take at best five to ten minutes but it would save ten times the time for the next day as you would just start working on the various agenda items next day morning. Your agenda at night concept would make you relaxed, good sleep tonight and would make you open your eyes next day morning with active, robust and bubbling personality because what you have to do next day is all that is contained in a piece of paper with the caption "Agenda at Night" and prepared by you the previous night.

The organized person you will be, the relaxed person you would be, best time management you will achieve, a stress free working you will find, more productivity you will achieve but only when you prepare your agenda at previous night. So, it is time for you now to take inspiration from the great legendry personality of Emerson and now start making a new habit of writing down your agenda tonight for the next day. Let it be a part of your routine habit, let it go into your blood, let it be taken as a regular pill before going to bed. I can assure you that the immense benefits which you will derive by this one single theme will make you a more organized person and the calmness of mind would be achieved by you because your mind is going to be stable for the next day as you have already jotted down what to do and what not to do for the next day.

While you prepare your agenda at night, let it be on one sheet of paper and let it contain all the important activities which you want to do next day. In this sheet of "Agenda at Night" also jot down some of the important telephones which you have to do and also some important work activities which you have to organize. The work sheet statement will be your personal guide and instructor to manage your next day in the most profitable manner. Do take time to review this agenda two – three times in a day. It is not a wastage of time but it is a very good from a practical angle. Do remember that for you time is a big constraint to enable you to carry out all the wish list of your activities for the day. But this habit of writing down agenda for the next day in advance on the previous night will really become your best friend to help you and guide you in the sphere of better management of the next day in a most scientific as well as productive manner. If you have never had the habit of writing agenda at the previous night, now is the time to make this a habit which will give you lots of rewards in the years to come. I would be happy to receive your miracle results which you will achieve in a guaranteed way if you develop the habit of writing agenda at night. Do write to me at my E Mail Address - slakhotia@satyam.net.in about your experience of writing down agenda at night for the next wonderful day. I hope this would change your life style for becoming a super successful person.

When we talk of agenda, the simple answer is just jot down. Yes why should you keep all your pending items in your head and soul? Just jot down. This is the real practical mantra to make you super successful. Apart from agenda, also develop the habit of jotting down the points of discussion at your just concluded business meet for future reference. Similarly, if you are going to attend and participate in a big business discussion, then it also makes a sense to jot down the important points which you would like to place on record at the business meet. Similar is also the situation if you want a collaboration from a collaborator. Write down the fine points on which you want a clarification. Write down the important things which you would like to clarify. If you are going to take a distributorship or sole distributorship of some product, then also it would make you a super successful person if you write down the important points and the terms of agreement which you would like to be incorporated in your MOU. It is also a good habit to develop the habit of sending down minutes of the business meet etc. Yes, please make it a habit to send out minutes of the business meet to your business associates as soon as possible so that there is no confusion on the various points which you have discussed and agreed to at the time of business discussion. I recollect couple of months ago when I was having a long chat with Narendra Verma, my publisher, we had met each other after a gap of long time. Hence, it was a very good opportunity for both of us to exchange notes and think on various vistas, visions, ideas, planning of the books to be written, language translation of various books and so on. We had along one to one some 70 minutes long non-stop discussion and also it was a non-interrupted discussion. I reached back my home. I thought that in a day or two when I am free, I will better jot down the summary of all that we have discussed for our remembrance. As I was to close the day, I was surprised to find a very detailed and exhaustive e-mail from Narendra Verma sending me minutes of the discussion which we had for 70 minutes. Each and every item of our discussion was clearly spelt out and this made my mind lighter. Just imagine Narendra Verma would not have sent me the detailed copy of the minutes and even if I would not have made my notes, then in the months to follow it was possible that some important points must have missed or that could also be a possibility of misunderstanding about the quantity of the publication, about the language edition and so on but I regard this type of idea of sending "Business Minutes" as a real practical idea for one's Supper success in business and to escape the missing out of some important point. It also brings on record the summary of all that transpired during the business meet. Hence, do make it a habit always to send minutes of business meetings as a routine part of your business action. If you make it a regular habit then surely some day you will be able to reap the great fruits of this idea.

16

Select your Stress busters if you want to attain Super Success

Super successful person should never be wedded to stress. The term stress should be completely out from the dictionary of a super successful person. However, the fact remains that when you are trying to reach the ladder of super success in your field or activity, stress is bound to be a part of the game. But do not give importance to stress but just think about the stress busters in your life. Yes, the super successful person you are, then surely it is you and you alone who will be now required to design your own stress busters. Although there is no standard set formula of the stress busters which can be taken advantage of to avoid and reduce the stress in you, but the fact remains that it all depends upon one's own liking. And this liking about a particular activity which may or may not be a part of your stress buster action plan.

All that is required to be done in the first place is only to agree to the theme that some type of stress buster has to be a part of your life style so that whenever you are under stress may be due to deadline for your activity or for any other matter, then you catch hold of these stress busters to remove the stress in you and again and again make you the real super successful person.

Innumerable stress relievers are on your mind self. It is you who should pick up one or two or even more stress busters which fit in your liking and which provide you stress free environment at a time when you are really stressed. In case you have a young child in your family, then surely spending five to fifteen minutes with this young child will absolve all your stress levels. Make it a habit of playing with the child two-three times minimum in a day to take off your stress. If someone feels interested in spirituality, he may think of resorting to reading a two page printed text of some good spiritual book which will take away his stress. In choosing a book try to think of such a book which is inspirational in nature so that when you are at reading of the book, your stress level gets controlled. Even think of reading inspiring quotations, inspiring anecdotes and inspiring lives of great men of the world. This type of reading will surely help you remove your stress level in the body. If you love music, then surely listening to light music of your choice is another real stress buster for you. You can even think of having a combination of three or four different activities which will help you in melting out the stress level in your day to day life. If nothing is found handy or you are in a fix as to what should your stress buster be, then it is time to calmly sit down, closing your eyes and just chanting the name of the Almighty for five minutes only. Believe me this is going to bring great relief to your stress level. If you want to achieve the best results and guaranteed results to control your stress through meditation, then just take out three to five minutes only, close your eyes, sit in any posture as you feel comfortable and just whisper silently the name of any God in which you have the faith. Supposing you are still confused about the name of the God, the name which is to be chanted, which is the best one, which brings the best and fast results for me, these types of pointers are coming in your mind, then just think of chanting *Om*. I assure all my readers that if they chant *Om* only for three to five minutes at a time, when they are in great stress, then they will come out very fast from the tunnel of stress and will be able to find themselves unstressed and blissful environment would be experienced by them; this is the great magic power of chanting the name of

God. If your work schedule is such that great stress becomes a part of your routine life style for the whole day, then surely you must resort to chanting of the name of God three to four times in a day. Yes, you can chant the name of God even for just sixty seconds and get relief from stressful atmosphere. There is no fixed posture or style in which the chanting of the name has to be done. Just remember you can chant the name of the God while you are sitting in the car or you are walking in the office or you are sitting on your chair. With my practical experience I can say that large number of people have been benefited by taking recourse to stress buster formula in the concept of chanting the holy name of the Almighty. Why not you? Try now. It would cost nothing but it helps instantly and immensely.

The simple point which I want to emphasise is that for real super successful person stress should never be a part of the life style. But if the work exigency is required or is making stress, then get ready in advance of the stress buster in your life. Don't copy cat the stress busters of your friends and relatives. But try to develop your own stress buster which shows it will become really effective to de-stress the stress in you. You will agree that no great work and no great thinking is possible at a time when you are stressed. Hence, it is always necessary that all super successful persons in the world should say good bye to stress by resorting to some sort of stress buster in their life. It is also recommended that you should share your own stress busters with your friends and may get some new ideas to beat the stress in you.

17

Passion and Passion to make your Super Success

Not merely a business tycoon but if you want to be a real celebrity star in the field of music, dance or acting, all that is needed is passion for your desired aim. Please do remember that unless and until you have a dedicated and devoted passion for your desired goal and aim in life, it is not possible for you to achieve super success either in business or in profession or in any other walk of life. Hence, passion is a very important phenomenon in which you must have great faith, respect and regard. The faith in passion can be seen when you really have a great passion for that particular activity. Whether it is day or whether it is night every time you must have your dedicated passion for a particular activity in which you are interested. Only then it will be possible for you to achieve super success in your life. When someone becomes the market leader let us say of steel industry not merely in a particular town or in a particular state or in whole of India but in whole of the world, then the answer is that because of the great passion that person might be having to become the steel king of the world. In the same manner, you must continue to have passion and not just forced time spending for your activity. If you are having a passion dedicated to your activity of your liking and you are devoted to that passion 24X7, still you will find that you never become tired or exhausted because it is that great passion which is responsible for making you a real super successful person and a super star in your activity, in your business, in your profession or in any other field which you choose. The story of Gillette is known to everyone. Mr. Gillette who had a great passion for inventing a razor that would be sharp and provide a clean shave and still not very costly and let it be thrown away and let it become a disposable razor. The dream was good and he taught it to make it sound idea into a profitable venture. He worked more than 48 months continuously and that work produced the first disposable razor and it took further 72 months to get that razor placed in the stores. In the first year the sale of blade was less than 100. But the passion was strong and it was that passion of Mr. Gillette that made his company as the number one company in the whole world for disposable shaving equipment. It was not just luck due to which Mr. Gillette found his success story but just it was his dedicated passion which made him successful in his venture. Similarly, is the story of Colonel Sanders who founded Kentuncky Fried Chicken (KFC). In the initial years he had been to thousand of places and to thousands of the prospective buyers and make them interested in his products and activities but no success. But it was his passion which won him the coveted results as desired by him.

Do remember that you too can achieve everything that you want only with dedicated passion or committed passion. If you are into committed passion, then surely nothing on the earth can stop you to make super success achievement in your life time itself. Hence, let committed passion be your inbuilt action plan for achieving your super success.

18

Financial Literacy for your Super Success

You may be a born entrepreneur or you may be a born musician or an artist or may be fashion designer. But the fact remains that if you want to achieve super success, then surely you must be financial literate. If you are successful, you might have amazed lot of wealth but if you are unable to control that wealth and manage that wealth in a most profitable manner, then you would be just termed as a successful person but never ever a super successful person. Hence, if you are to be a super successful personality in the field in which you are interested, then surely financial literacy should be a part of your main agenda.

Sometimes all those with no Commerce or Finance background feel that how it is possible for us to develop financial literacy because we have never in the past had any occasion or a specialized learning to become financial literate. Just remember that you can be a real super success achiever in life in your life in the matter of handling your finances. Thus, even if you have never had any knowledge or idea of different financial products and of different tax related financial matters etc., don't worry at all. A super successful person never worries but only starts learning what he does not know. So we have to be definitely financially literate, investment literate, tax literate to enable us to come out from the arena of success into the arena of super success. It is worthwhile watching at least for half an hour every day the Business TV

Channel so as to get the latest update on the changing market trend and also to understand more about share, the stock market, real estate matters etc., etc. I can say with confidence that by now crores of people throughout India are regularly watching my TV Show known as Tax Guru which I present every week on CNBC Awaaz. All those persons who would like to possess financial literacy in the field of income-tax matters concerning the tax payment and also concerning their tax saving can develop the regular habit of watching this TV Serial sitting in their residence and thus they can be tax wise literate. Similarly, different shows are presented by different TV channels which can help a person to learn more and more about various aspects concerning financial matters which ultimately will help him in the process of his becoming a super successful personality.

Now-a-days most of the knowledge is available free of cost on the internet. What is all needed is only your thought process to take a decision that yes you need financial literacy and once you make it an item on which to concentrate, then surely your financial literacy will make you super successful person particularly in the field of your business, trade or industry. I recollect last year I had done special TV show for couple of top film stars and media personality who were participating in Amitabh Bachchan's show, *The Bigg Boss Reality Show.* I was doing a special programme on TV known as *The Big M Show.* In this TV Show I was talking to these media personalities and film stars and film heroines about money management matters connected with them. I would like to place on record that most of the successful film personalities were not devoting much time to the aspects connected with financial literacy but as they learnt and heard about the utility and importance of financial literacy. So my dear friends, please note that if you want to be a super successful person, never ever ignore financial literacy from your mind block.

19

Depression and Anxiety out from the dictionary of Super Successful persons

You are depressed, you are gloomy and in these moments you don't feel like talking to anyone. You are sitting calm and quite. While you are depressed, your creative energy also gets depressed. Your mood is out of the track due to depression and because of this, your personality gets a big blow. You wanted to be a super successful person. You are not able to become a successful person just because depression is surrounding your personality. Similar is also the theme with regard to anxiety. Carry out your activity with the blessing of the Almighty God but never be excited. Too much happiness or too much pleasure or happening of an event should not make you excited. Likewise too much big loss or big business problem should also not make you exciting or worried. The best formula for a super successful person is never to be depressed and never to show the signs of anxiety.

Depression is a part of life. The theme for a super successful person is how then to cope up with depression. Although these days good number of medicines are available to take you out from the arena of depression but I personally feel that self help techniques and ideas will help you to do away your depression. Hence, if you are working in the direction of becoming a super successful person, make sure that you delete depression and anxiety from your personality frame. You should be depression-free always and that you should also never be an excited or agitated person. A person who is excited or agitated or even depressed reflects these qualities on his own personality and thus takes him away from becoming a super successful person.

The practical tip for a depressed person is that he should cut away his connections from those activities and those persons coming nearer to whom he gets depressed. Always continue to think and ponder and think and jump to the conclusion that super successful person you have to become and with the heavy load of anxiety as well as depression you surely cannot become a super successful person.

20

Never, ever pay attention to what others will say

If you just keep your eyes and ears open to what others are saying about you, about your dressing sense, about your car, about your habit, then soon you will think that you are not a person with holistic exposure. Hence, never, ever pay attention to what others will say about you. Right now you are travelling in an old Maruti car. Most of your colleagues and friends, they are driving the costly cars. You are still staying in a rented premises while your colleagues have taken good apartments which they have purchased by a bank loan. If these types of situation exists then you feel that what others will say about me if I stay in a shabby locality or if I use an old car, then a sort of inferiority complex will enter your mind. Therefore, a person with one single aim and mission of being a super successful person should never, ever pay attention to what others are thinking about him and his living style. You too should never pay attention to what others speak about your living style and other connected matters. At best you can have introspection review the way in which you are living but never be affected by what others say. Similarly, never, ever spend more money just to become a stylish person and interesting personality in the eyes of your friends and relatives. Always go on doing what all that you think is good and proper looking to your facts, situation and circumstances. If you adhere to this formula, you will have no problem in being a super successful person.

21

Love someone and tell someone

For a super successful person it is necessary that he or she should love someone from the core of his heart and also should find at least one such person to whom he can tell everything without any barriers. It is true that it is very difficult these days to find relatives and friends to whom you can open out your heart. But if you make a sincere effort and try, it will be possible for you to find out such person before whom you can open out your heart at any point of time and speak out to such person everything that you have in your mind. Please do remember that for a super successful person it is necessary that your mind and your heart is always clean and pure. It is not surrounded by problems caused by whatsoever reason. Hence it is time for you now to love someone and try to identify a person whom you can speak out your heart. With effort from your side it will be possible for you to find at least one or two such persons whom you can share everything of your personal life. To find this type of a person the first point that you should consider is that you should try to become such a person on whom other person can rely as his best friend on the earth and that your friend should speak out his mind without any hesitation. When such is the situation, then in your mutual interest you will surely find the guy to whom you can tell everything on earth and similarly that guy is also able to speak out to you.

22

Gearing up for challenges

A super successful person is always ready and geared up to face any challenge of the life. Hence, if you want to be a real super successful person, then do remember that be ready always to face the challenges of the life as they come. It is a fact that any new activity or any new innovative initiative which you will like to start will not come to you handy. You have to face the challenges of life and it is only all those who are able to face the challenges of life that they become real super successful persons. The theme of gearing up for facing the challenges is applicable in every sphere of life, be it a business activity or be it the starting of a social organization. I recollect that one person being inspired by Lions Club International and the Rotary Club International thought of starting another International Organisation exclusively for ladies. The idea was unique. But what was needed was the dashing push for the challenges which come in between the start of new club activity. This is how Soroptimist International was born. This is a global organization of professional women with nearly one lakh members in 123 countries of the world. In India already Soroptimist International is having presently 14 such clubs spread in different parts of India. Various social projects are also undertaken by this new International Organisation. The fact is that in every walk of life the super successful person is ready to face the challenges and is never afraid of facing such challenges. So my dear friends, if you are aiming to become a super successful person, then do always welcome the challenges which come in your life. I recollect the excellent story of a big developer in real estate. I met him about 10-12 years ago. At that time he was just a real estate broker and now it is just because of his ability to gear up for facing the challenges in life that he has developed a very big enterprise of Real Estate Development. His real estate activities are now being carried out in different parts of India and he had also successfully launched a big Public Issue of his Real Estate Company. Well this can be possible even for you. But only what is needed is that you should gear up to face the challenges of life as they come in every walk at every time. And then you see no going back and you are transformed into a super successful personality.

23

Innovation: The key to your Super Success

All those who are interested to achieve super success will have to keep in mind one point at every point of time and that is innovation and innovation. If you are in business, you make profit. But you do not pay attention to further increase your business with innovative vistas and ideas. Then definitely, you cannot achieve future prosperity. Hence, please do remember that innovation is the key to your super success. Let us take the example of Maruti Car. Maruti Car started production nearly 26 years ago and in the initial year 1983-84 the capacity of Maruti Car Company was just 843 cars in a year and now 26 years later they are going to roll out 10 lakh cars in a year. The super success story of Maruti Car is because of the innovative style in which it has been functioning. Constant product development, design development, new products launching are all part of the innovative style to carry on business activities which have made Maruti a super successful business venture in last 26 years. New fresh ideas come to you for your business or profession and let innovative skill and visions be introduced by you from time to time to make you the real super successful person. Throughout the world in this present technological age a bunch of young bubbling entrepreneurs are exploring new innovations and new ideas in their money making vision. One of the young business entrepreneur just because of his innovative skills thought of an idea to combine the convenient of digital photography v.

the charm of traditional photo albums into a lucrative business model. Similarly another young talented youth taking a clue from Talent Hunt Shows on television thought of starting a Talent Show and have been successful because of his innovative idea. Likewise one another young entrepreneur has appreciated the power of collective bargaining over internet and for that purpose a new business venture has come into existence relating to innovative bargaining of net products through bulk buying group. Please do remember that innovation is the key to your super success. Hence, in whatever activity you are, always think of innovative ideas and innovative skills which alone will be responsible to make you a super successful person.

One should never think of that how can I with my limited resources, with my little limited knowledge etc. can create innovation. Never think on these lines. A live example is of one Prasanta Barik who started as a domestic help in Delhi. He studied only up to Class VIII. He was working as Office Assistant and now in Delhi and he is being invited in literary festival and poetry reading session. Well this is something which you will not believe. But believe me when I say that this Prasanta, the domestic help, has now written 9 books on poetry and they have been published, he also has short stories to his credit too and now he is invited by Poetry Clubs and other organizations. The theme is that it is innovation which brings you super success in your life.

Similarly, the great American singer Christina likes to read books with erotic content. This great American singer would like to read novel while she is soaking in foam. Well this is a reality come true not just a joke. This fact is being reported by femalefirst.co.uk. Well, the love of this great American singer is to read erotic stories while taking a bath. Your next question may be how can one take a bath and read books also. It was some super successful person who had thought to create water proof books full of erotic stories. Yes, it is this great innovation of some super successful person which has made it possible for the American singer Christina to read the book while taking a bath and that the book does not get wet.

Innovative person will make super success in any field in which he is into. For example in already crowded San Francisco Town of USA on the roof top of a tall building in Down Town area where you can see a number of restaurants already running. But there is a restaurant called Cheese Gay Factory. This Cheese Gay Factory is famous as it provides food bites of a bigger size. It is true that the innovation in serving the food in America is that Food Bites in America are getting bigger and bigger and the customer is happy and the sales are high and this innovative idea has helped the owner to achieve super success. We all know that in America everything is bigger and bigger. America has long broad open land where one can see everything on a big scale whether it is the big sky or the big plain land or the big houses or even the big cars and the big roads. And now finally the size of your dinner plate and the dinner itself is very big. The quantity of the dinner dish is big too. This I call as the innovative style and it is this innovative style that results into super success of a person. Likewise we see the new Township Development and in different parts of the world. However, I am very much amazed to see the innovative development of the city of Lavasa which is being designed with the help of the world's greatest architect. The innovation with which the city of Lavasa is being built is soon going to see it flourish as a remarkable and wonderful destination. Thus, innovation helps you to achieve super success in whatever field you are. Lavasa however, is easily accessible from Mumbai and Pune and the Lavasa project under development is across 100 sq. km. Just think of this innovative vista of developing a complete new town which would be almost ¼ of the size of Mumbai town would make for their promoters super successful achievement just because of innovative vision and style which is away from the routine work of setting up a township.

In any field if you want super success, then definitely innovation is the key word. It is innovation which will definitely bring prosperity and super success to your project. For example when we talk of travel, we find that nearly half a century old Sandy Lane Beach resort happens to be one of the finest resort in the Caribbean. This resort is situated in Saint James in the Island nation of Barbados and definitely it happens to be one of the greatest retreat for all those with jaded nerves and stress at their back. The Sandy Lane Beach Resort has been voted as world's number one travel destination. This resort has been the preferred resort of a large number of celebrities and some of the biggest names in business. It was way back in the year 1961 that the promoters of this beach resort thought of innovative idea and now it is ultimate haven of luxury. The resort was demolished nearly ten years ago and later on it was remodeled and re-prepared. One of the biggest moments of celebration for the owners of this resort was a time when in the year 2004 Tiger Woods hosted his marriage ceremony at the Golf Club attached to this great resort and the Golf Club was designed by Golfer Tom Fazio. Another special feature of this resort is that it can boast of world's best destination spa.

Apart from great Cuisine, it is the innovative style of working that makes Warren Buffet, the America's most famous investor. At a time when the recession is there in the economy Buffet uses this recession to amess assets. He is of the view that a climate of fear is investors best friend. Hence, if you are aiming for your super success, then surely take a clue from all those super achievers about the innovative manner in which they handle their business matters.

If you are sailing in the turbulent market, it is time now for the super successful person to attend the Top Premier Business Leaders Conferences and Conventions. These conferences and conventions where you will find a host of renowned speakers and once you listen to them about their thoughts and understanding business in the turbulent time, then surely your capacity to fight the turbulent times in the markets gets geared up. Hence, innovate your idea of getting skill by attending business leaders forums and business summits which are conducted throughout the world. It is time now to make your connections and unlock opportunities through participating in the business conferences, seminars even talk shows. Attend the top business shows for your inner strength and for getting at least some innovative ideas which alone can bring you super success in the years to come.

24

Never be an egocentric person

The making of you as a super successful person can get shattered if you are an egocentric person. Hence, when you are contemplating for your super success, never let ego rule you, rule the wisdom of your mind. Never ever dream of destroying the wonderful gracious world of bliss and happiness by your egocentric attitude in life. Never, therefore, let ego come in your way. However, in the first place ask yourself a small little simple question – "Are you an egoistic person?" Well, most of the readers would say, "Oh! How can you tell me an egoistic person?" But the fact is that if you calmly and coolly sit down for just few minutes, you will be able to find the real you in your personality and then may be you come to the conclusion that yes, you are an egoistic person. But don't worry. Don`t be afraid. Don`t be scared even if you are an egoistic person today. Just think that it is the good quality in you that you want to remove and do away with your egoistic attitude in life. The thought about doing away with your egoistic personality itself is the right direction to make you wonderful and fruitful personality in the years to come. Shed your ego attitude. You may think that why should you when others don't. These are the pointers that might come in your mind. But then, don`t worry. Think over them. Think that egoistic attitude takes away the super successful personality of yours. Hence, just because you want to achieve super success, it is time now for you to do away completely your egoistic vision and egoistic thinking.

25

Love your work to remove fatigue and become a super successful person

If you love your work, you don't get tired. This is really an experience which cannot be found in books. But this is an experience which can be felt, which can be experienced by one and all. Whatever work you are doing, if you do that work with love towards that work, then your fatigue would be a thing of the past. Long back Will Rogers said that if you want to be successful, it is just a simple formulae : 'Know what you are doing. Love what you are doing and believe in what you are doing'. With my experience I can say that what Will Rogers said long back is true in the present context. Rather I would say love what you are doing as you reach the path of super success.

'I slept and dreamt that life was joy. I woke and saw that life was duty. I acted and behold, duty was joy'. These are the golden words spoken by Rabindra Nath Tagore 150 years ago. But the theme is very interactive even today to make you a super successful person. Love your work. Get joy from your work to avoid the fatigue and to become a super successful person.

Specially when a person reaches his golden year of birth he starts experiencing down-trend in physical activity and also starts feeling fatigue in all the work he is engaged in. As and when fatigue approaches the work he attributes it solely to the age factor. But the fact remains that age is not at all a contributory factor in causing fatigue to a person. If a person loves his work then fatigue will be washed away. Recently while I was in a Doctor's clinic waiting for my turn to come I found that the face of the receptionist at the Reception counter was full of cheerfulness. It was 7.00 P.M. in the evening and this receptionist was a person of nearly 65 years of age. I would see the same person whenever I visited the Doctor's clinic, whether it was at 9.00 P.M. or some times even later at 7.00 P.M. All the day all the time I would see this man with the sparkling cheerfulness on his face on all the days all the time. The other day while I was waiting in the Doctor's clinic for my turn to come I just walked near this old cheerful gentleman and asked him as to what was the reason of his being cheerful all the time on all the days. Did he ever see any glooming time in his life? With the cute little smile he just said, "I love my work and that is the sole reason that keeps me cheerful all the time on all the days". My next question to him was that as he was 65 he must be feeling tired or bored with his work especially with long working hours from 9.00 A.M. to 7.00 P.M. and for 6 days a week. His answer was, never in his life he felt tired or bored. Again with yet another cute smile his answer was, "It is just because that I love my work that I enjoy my work which keeps me happy and fresh all the time on all the days". Yes, it is a reality that if you love the work you don't get tired. Reversely, if a person does not love his work and does the work with a grim face and without cheerfulness and feeling burden of the work or having a feeling of what ordinary type of work or routine type of work he has to do then you will find that he becomes tired and cheerfulness becomes a thing of the past. Thus, what is recommended is that all those persons who are interested to do work without getting tired and without experiencing fatigue of the work should always ensure that they do the work with real love towards the work. This is the only success formula of doing the work without getting tired.

26

Control your emotions and let not emotions control you

Emotions. Yes, being a human person with a brain and a soul it is true that you will have your emotions. Each person has his own emotions. But it is only those who are super successful persons that they control their emotions and that they do not permit their emotions to control them. If you take this lesson right now today, then you will find that your role to super success will not be damaged at any point of time. In my last 42 years of interaction in the public meetings with cross section of the people of different castes, colours, society and religion coming from different corners of the world, I found that not controlling of these emotions lead you to your destruction. You are likely to fall in the well of frustration, anguish and become unsuccessful person just because you have not been able to control your emotion. It is the practical intelligent handling of your emotions that help you to reach the ladder of super success. In business, in social circle, in family life, everywhere you are required to control your emotions. Don't get agitated, Don't get angry, don't get frustrated, don't speak out your mind unless it is needed. This is known as controlling your emotions. Enjoy the world as it comes. Emotion will make your mind disturbed at some point of time. But those emotions require a brake. Just as road accidents are avoided due to intelligent use of the brake, in the same manner your super successful personality cannot be ruined if you resort to the concept of controlling your emotions and let not emotions control you.

27

Genuine help to one and all

If you want to become a super successful person then do extend a genuine hand to help one and all at all times. It is a fact that when you are ready to extend genuine help, assistance and guidance to all those who need it then you become darling of all and it is the quality of a super successful person. Do develop not only the quality but also the principle of extending genuine help and be one among those persons who are part of a super successful family.

28

Reading makes a complete Super Successful man

Way back the great philosopher of the 15th century Francis Bacon said that 'reading makes a full man, conference a ready man, and writing an exact man'. Although these great words were narrated by Francis Bacon more than 500 years ago, but even today his dictum is a source of success for all those who would like to be super successful persons because the habit of reading would definitely make you a full man. And it is only when you are a full man, then you can achieve super success. It is time now that you inculcate the reading habit in yourself and also inspire all young boys and girls in particular to develop this habit of reading. Do take out some time from your daily schedule to keep on reading - reading for knowledge, reading for mental change, reading for introspection of your own life and reading to get inspiration from what others have done. In case you are busy most of the time and you fail to find any time for general reading then do always carry a book with you which you can first start reading while you are waiting at the airport or railway station or in the alternate take time to read after you have checked in at the airport. In case you are traveling in a car obviously you can get lot of time to carry out your reading habit.

29

Concentration of your mind for your brilliant success

A super successful person must have such a mind which happens to be under his control all the time. The mind should be focused. The mind should be brilliant. The mind should be dynamic. The mind must produce something new always. The mind should never feel tired. All these are great virtues for becoming a super successful person. Well, if you really want your mind to be a real vibrant mind, then it is time for you now to think of concentration of the mind. Yes, by regular practice and keen desire you can achieve your goal of concentrating your mind. Long ago *Katha Upanishad* said that he who is possessed of supreme knowledge by concentration of his mind, must have his senses under control, like spirited steeds control by charioteer. It is a well-known fact that our Upanishads are the words of wisdom coming from the Almighty God. If you can have inspiration from the above dictum of Upanishad, then surely you will be able to have the development of your mind and the developed mind can be transferred into a concentrated mind. A concentrated mind will always bring in better fruits for you in every walk of your life.

If we talk of studies, then surely if you are having a concentrated mind, it will help you to achieve the best in your studies. It will improve your result and it will bring you on the list of topmost students of your class, the school and the university. Likewise, if you are in business, your concentrated mind will help you to excel in business in comparison with other business associates. Similarly, if you are a professional person, a lawyer in particular, then the concentrated mind will help you argue in a most focused manner before the judges. Hence, it is of utmost importance that you develop the habit of concentration of the mind.

Question now arises as to how to concentrate mind. The only answer for concentration of the mind is to meditate daily. This one medicine which we call as the medicine of meditation if taken up religiously every day, then surely it will help you to increase your concentration power of the mind. Once the mind is focused and concentrated, you will be able to remember much more, you will be able to redefine your thinking and you will be able to present your focused view point at a given gathering. Nothing special is needed for developing the theme of concentration of the mind. When we talk of meditation from the perspective of mind concentration, the simple activity is to just sit down in very calm and quiet corner of your house but at a fixed time to reap the best results and then close your eyes and meditate 5 to 10 minutes. Gradually every month increase your meditation by just 5 minutes. If you are able to extend your meditation, say upto 30 minutes a day, then you will yourself see the difference in the merit power of your own mind which has been possible only due to the concentration of your mind. Hence, start doing right now the practice of meditation and make it a part of your daily routine agenda. Initially when you start meditating, then there will come in your mind not one or two but hundreds of thoughts of different items, ideas, your pending agenda, your tensions and everything else and all that you are doing on the earth. However, let all these activities and actions come and then go and again come but again go. Just close your eyes, sit down coolly and calmly in a relaxed atmosphere and let it all happen as it happens. Do not take any special efforts to control the thoughts that come in your mind. Thoughts will come but will also go instantly also. Do not ever make effort to erase these thoughts. The thoughts will be erased automatically in due course and then you will find in your mind that your mind has attained the height of being a concentrated mind which you will experience by meditation in next 15 days only. Let focused meditation of your mind regularly result into concentration of your mind.

30

Apologise instantly

It is the quality of the super successful man that he is always ready to apologise instantly for his mistake etc. Hence, if you want to be a super successful person in your life, then do adopt this virtue of always being ready to tender apology in case of any mistake etc. It also shows a great character of yours once you adopt this theme.

I remember that recently in our foreign tour to Finland, we had a guide who was not very mature one. He would argue with the tour group on small little matters. He would not understand the language of courtesy and was not at all in the habit of extending apology for the small little lapses on his part. Anyway, after three days of our tour, I explained him the magic power of extending apology. Now, he was charmed with my suggestion and soon he changed his attitude and now in the next eleven days of our tour we all had a wonderful time just because of change in the attitude of our tour guide whereby the art of extending apology magic really played.

31

Be a good listener

The art of listening to others is a great art to make you a super successful person. Hence, whenever someone is talking to you, do listen what he is saying with apt attention. Sometimes we find that during the course of our business or profession or even social interaction, we do not listen very carefully to what the other person is saying. Hence, it is always a good theme to be a good listener. I recollect my grandfather late Shri Mohan Lalji Lakhotia, way back nearly 30 years ago while having his regular morning walk, was an apt listener to all the morning walkers. It is this quality that made him very popular amongst the company of highly intellectual persons who were regular walkers in the past. Although my grandfather was educated just up to Class IV but it was his immensely good habit of being a good listener that made him so popular. Therefore, try to become always a good listener. Just don't be a good listener but become a genuine listener. I have met many wonderful persons who pretended as if they were listening but actually they were not. Hence, always be a genuine listener , if somebody is telling a story do not just interrupt in between even if you know the story, as it is bad manner which always should be avoided by the super successful person.

32

Impulses are not good for your super success.

It is a well-known fact that impulses generally are neither good nor generally are bad. It is all how we use such impulses that make them good or bad. Hence, a super successful person should always learn to use his impulses for good and wonderful work. A person who has controlled his impulses is alone a super successful person. Such a person is bound to be religious, calm and quiet and can be said to be qualified in highest educational field. Hence, always try to develop your character in such a manner that impulses are not a problem for you. However, do not be an impulsive buyer. Likewise, on your pleasure trip in case you happen to visit Casino then impulsive playing should be avoided at every cost.

33

Practical spirituality for practical super success

All those who are interested to achieve super success in their life must plan always to be a part of super spirituality in their day-to-day life. Practical spirituality in nutshell demands always to be good, always to be kind and always love one another as also to take care of everyone whom you meet. If you are really adopting practical spirituality, then it is also time for you now to spurn your desires, do remember that only when you spurn your desire, you are nearer to God and this is an act of practical spirituality.

Practical spirituality in a holistic manner would do good advantage in many ways in making you a real super successful person. For achieving practical spirituality the starting point should be to understand the meaning and the importance of this theme. Believe me, the concept of Practical Spirituality adopted by you is going to really help you achieve your own super success and provide you great benefits and bring peace in you–all the day, all the time.

34

Stimulate your knowledge

A super successful man at every point of time in life stimulates his knowledge and this stimulation of the knowledge is not merely in respect of knowledge required for ones own business or profession but the horizon of stimulating your knowledge should go a step forward and one should acquire more and more knowledge in different walks of life. I would like to remind our readers the golden words with regard to knowledge stimulation as per Bertrand Russel. He used to say, "Mere intellectual knowledge has no motivation of its own : the source of it stimulating their knowledge power. is in the field of emotion and sentiments in man. Something must stimulate knowledge, otherwise it will remain static and unable to influence human action." Thus, super successful persons in different corners of the world always aim at stimulating their knowledge power.

35

Enjoy life every moment

One should enjoy life and this enjoyment should not be for a particular day or a particular month or on the happening of a particular event. However, the best super successful persons always enjoy life and they enjoy every moment of the life. It is time for you and for me and for everyone to enjoy every moment of our life. If you keep in your mind the theme of enjoying every moment of your life, then surely will come nearer to holistic enjoyment and the enjoyment will become a part of your routine daily. Hence, start enjoying every moment of life. Always think that it is through the blessing of the Almighty God that you are able to enjoy life at this moment.

36

Love one another – always

No ill feeling, no agitation but complete love for each and every human being you meet– is the secret of a super successful person. Love one another – always and in all situations. This motto is the key to keep us a part of our life's super success formula, then surely the life will become really more wonderful for everyone.

37

A small is beautiful

Generally speaking, people want big and big alone. You want big car, you want big name and you want big money. However, I believe always in the great dictum of Mother Teresa who used to say that 'small is beautiful'. Long back nearly thirty years ago I had met Mother Teresa at a Tea Party at Governor House, Kolkata. In my brief and short exclusive meeting with Mother Teresa when I wanted her to write some message for me she wrote – "Small is beautiful". I always believe that small things are really beautiful and hence one should extend small courtesies, small charities and small little help which one can offer to another person. In making super successful person of you these habits of extending small assistance, help, guidance etc. to different people whom you meet in different walks of life really aim to make you a real super successful person.

38

Don't ever be surprised by realities of life

In different walks of life and at different intervals you will come across different activities happening in your life. Sometimes you will be shocked to find that the most trusted friend, the most trusted business associate and the most trusted relative has gone against your desired wishes and emotions. Hence, one should never be surprised by the real hard facts of life and one should face it as it comes.

39

Live In Today (LIT)

Don't think of yesterday. Don't think of tomorrow but only think of today. Yes, this single mantra will help you to overcome many small problems which may come in your life because what all you are required to do is only to live in today. Never live in the past and never also live in the future years to come. Think today as a bliss from the Kingdom of God and just develop the habit of living in today only.

40

Search opportunity from adversity

The super successful person is ever ready to grab new opportunities in life. These opportunities may be in the sphere of business or profession or in the sphere of service career or may be in other walks of life. But the fact remains that all those who are super successful persons are always ready to hunt for opportunities in their life. Grab the opportunities when it comes and also do remember whenever there is a chaos either in your family life or be it in your business or professional life or the chaos may be in your service career, it is at such point of time when the chaos is being faced by you that you are able to find a golden opportunity for your super success. Hence, whenever there is a chaos in a given situation, just sit down calmly and coolly and just think of the best action plan which can be implemented in such a situation. Who knows the chaos in your life may turn into an opportunity for you!

41

You should know how to read the balance sheet of life

It is not merely in business or profession that you need to prepare the balance sheet containing the list of the assets and the liabilities of your life on a particular given date. However, all super successful persons always read the balance sheet of their life. A businessman's balance sheet contains the details of all his assets and so also his liabilities. Similarly prepare the balance sheet of your life and take regular time out from your busy schedule to read the balance sheet not of your financial matters but the balance sheet of your real life. In this balance sheet of your life prepare the assets which you possess and in the liabilities write down your shortcomings. Review this balance sheet at regular intervals. Do remember it is this non-materialistic balance sheet which will bring lot of peace and bliss to you and it will help you to make a super successful person.

42

Deserve v. desire – your path to happiness

Those who are not merely successful but super successful in their walks of life, they have got several desires which require to be fulfilled by them. It is nothing wrong to think of some desires and then ultimately to aim at putting in best of yours to achieve these desires. However, in practical parlance we find that in real life many of our desires in spite of our best efforts are not fulfilled. In such a situation, a person may get disturbed, perturbed and may face uneasiness. Well, at such point of time, the super successful persons do not ever think about the repercussions of their unfulfilled desires. But they have great faith in the dictum of the Almighty namely deserve v. desire. At that point of time in life when you find that your desired goals are not achieved, then you should just think that it is the Almighty's desire to grant me not what I desire but what I deserve. This type of thinking if you have in your mind, then you will be able to find a wonderful path of happiness for you.

43

Secluded quarterly introspection

Let quarterly introspection be a part of your routine life. Sit down couple of hours every quarter in a silent place just with a plain piece of paper and a pen. Let no other thoughts come in between while you are having your regular quarterly introspection. The best theme of quarterly introspection is to have it done in a secluded area where complete bliss and peace of mind is at your doorstep and you are able to concentrate on judicial thinking of different aspects of your own life, the mission, the aim, the failures, the success and so on. At this quarterly introspection you should review not merely your business or profession or your service career but you should equally review your social activities, your role towards relatives, your role towards the family and the children and thus you should have a holistic quarterly introspection which will bring more happiness and will focus your mind to achieve fuller goals in life.

44

Let your motto be– Your Trust, our Pride

Each person must prepare a motto. Think not once but hundred times to finalise your motto. However, once the motto is finalised, then stick to it. I feel that for all those persons who want to achieve super success in life, the real motto for them should be that 'ethics is good business'. I remember on the occasion of Century anniversary celebrations of the very famous Chamber of Commerce of New Delhi namely the PHD Chamber of Commerce they took a motto of 'ethics is good business'. Similarly I believe that if you keep your motto as trust on you by your customers and that happens to be a pride for you.

45

Don't be weak emotionally

This is my dictum and my way of dealing with day to day emotions of life. This single message has been instrumental in making change in the lives of a large number of top corporate executives and have enabled them to become super successful persons in their own field. Believe me when I say that it is definitely a must for every person to control his emotions and one should never be emotionally weak at any point of time under any given circumstance.

46

Write your book of dreams

Those who would like to become super successful persons, they should have a diary in which they should write down different dreams which come up in their mind from time to time. Yes, it is a very good habit to write down your dream as and when it comes to your mind because you do not know which dream you have been dreaming might become the king of your dreams. Ideas come, welcome each and every idea. Dreams similarly come, when they come receive it with warmth and capture such dreams in the pages of your diary. Not merely should you capture the dreams of your life but you should review such dreams at least once a month. Take time from your busy schedule once a month at least to read the dream book of yours.

47

PA for your super success

PA, I do not mean the Personal Assistant in your office at your command and control. What I mean is my concept of PA which means Positive Attitude (PA) for your super success. Always have positive attitude in life. Never think of any negativity at all. Be it with reference to business, inter personal relations, the family, the friends, the society or any other subject matter. Always have the habit of maintaining positive attitude at all times.

48

Say a big no to anxiety

Anxiety should be avoided at all times and specially by all those persons who want to achieve super success in life. Anxiety takes away good portion of your creativity. Similarly anxiety also takes away good amount of your time which otherwise you could have used it for completing some of your pending task. Hence, avoid anxiety at all times. If you keep anxiety on the top of your mind and body, then surely breakdown would be existing very soon for your health. Hence, if you want quality work done by you not to be hampered and if you want quality life, then anxiety should be avoided. We have seen many people unable to control anxiety and this results into full day wastage of their life cycle. Anxiety also makes the mind polluted. It weakens the mind. It takes away thinking about creativity. Hence, avoid anxiety always.

49

Think yourself as a precious jewel

Ask yourself a question, a small little question, "Am I a jewel"? Well, if you really ask this question standing just opposite the mirror in your room to yourself and no one listens to your answer, then you may just end up saying that not at all. I am not a jewel at all. Never, never think that you are not a jewel. Rather think that you are a jewel. Have faith in your self, think that you are a jewel and you will become.

50

Coping with uncertainties of future

If you can develop the quality of facing the uncertainties of future, then you are a real super successful person. Please do remember that the future uncertainties which are definitely going to happen and come in your life are really not known to anyone. They may come. They may not come. But still if you go on worrying about the future uncertainties in life, then your creative energy gets lost. Hence, it is time now for you to think always positive and not to ponder about uncertainties in the years to follow. Just remember if something wrong is going to happen, it will happen. You cannot stop it from happening. But you can definitely control the same by not worrying right now specially when some uncertainty today has not yet taken place. Hence, intelligent persons who would like to make a success in their life are always ready to cope up with the forthcoming uncertainties of life.

51

Security checking of your food

You must have heard about security checking be it at the airport or at the mall or at the hotel. But you might have never thought or heard about security checking of your food. Well, for becoming super successful you must always be in robust health. 'Health is Wealth'. That should be the motto. To achieve good health the answer is that you must constantly continue to have a security check of all the food which you eat. Hence, hygienic food should be your top priority because a wrong food taken by you will bring ill health and destroy your creativity.

52

Happiness factory - Your road to super success

In real life you may be having innumerable vistas which may bring super success. But please do remember that you must always continue to run your happiness factory at all times. If you are happy, you enjoy the work and you are not tired. This is the reality of life. I would also like to suggest to all those who would like to become super successful in their life to maintain a happiness diary for each day of the year. My suggestion given to large number of corporate houses specially to their CEOs and CFOs has worked wonders. I have suggested to the top elite executives of India to develop the habit of maintaining happiness diary. You can also start maintaining happiness diary for bliss, peace, happiness. The formula is very simple. Just take one blank diary. Write on each page the date and month. That is just allot one page for each day of the year. Now on the centre of the page draw a line. In the left side of the page put the heading "Happiness Pointers" while on the right hand side put the heading "Unhappiness Pointers". Now when you go to sleep before that just take out five minutes from your busy schedule and complete writing this happiness diary. In the column which states Happiness Pointers jot down all the points which provided you happiness during the day. Similarly, in another column with the caption Unhappiness Pointers also jot down all those pointers which during the day came in your life and provided unhappiness. Now finally close the day and close the Happiness Diary by giving marks for the day. That is you now judge your happiness for today. Give the marks from 10. If you achieve 5 plus marks in a day in favour of Happiness Pointers, then definitely you can think your life is smooth. If however, you receive less than five marks for a day for Happiness Pointers, then definitely something is wrong which requires to be corrected. The aim, however, should be to achieve 7 plus marks during each day of the year towards Happiness Pointers. Thus, if you maintain this happiness Diary, then the big advantage is that you can yourself judge the quantum of your happiness on daily basis and in case the happiness falls short of the desired results, then you can think upon to improve the happiness graph of your life. This happiness diary would do wonders for you. You can also buy this happiness diary published by Diamond Books.

53

Amazing calmness of mind and body

Mind should be completely calm at every point of time of the day and night. If you are able to control your mind with amazing calmness, it will provide you peace and will help you in the path of attaining happiness. Important business-related decisions and important business thinking can be achieved much faster, if you are able to control your mind by keeping it calm and cool always. Best examples of calmness of the mind can be seen in the lives of top surgeons of the world. They have always kept their mind calm and quiet. Only then, they are able to perform the surgery with precision and perfection. Hence, all super successful persons in life always resort to having continued calmness in their mind and body to enable them to achieve super success.

54

Commit mistakes, admit them but don't commit again

As we walk through different phases in life, we are bound to commit mistakes. But don't be perturbed or disturbed by the mistakes which you commit in your life. Sometimes it may even happen that after a particular mistake has been committed, you may feel yourself very guilty about that and sometimes you may say in your mind to yourself, "Oh what a silly mistake I have made". But don't worry at all for making mistakes. My simple formula is that if a mistake is made, have the courage to admit your mistake and do not commit the same type of mistake again. If we adopt this formula, this mantra, then definitely we will march ahead much faster to the ladder of super success.

55

Maintain Silence for 24 hours in a year

When you want to achieve your super success in your life, you can think of taking out 24 hours at least once in a year for experiencing the magic of silence. You may find it impractical to find time for keeping a complete 24 hours silence. This is a wonderful idea which in the first place I had experienced it and then with my own experience I got so much attached to this idea of 24 hours complete silence. I am inspired for this by the Father of the Nation, Mahatma Gandhi. Gandhiji used to have a 24 hour complete Maun that is silence every week. Even if foreign dignitaries would visit his Ashram, he would not talk to them at all on every Monday. Gandhiji would write and communicate even with the celebrities of the world. What Gandhiji used to practise once a week same principle I would be happy if you practise once a year at least. Complete silence implies that from 6 A.M. in the morning to the next day 6 A.M. you have to be silent. You can not talk to anyone. You can continue all your work may it be writing or reading or internet related activities and all activities including the viewing of TV or the picture show etc. But what you do not do is talking and talking. Let complete silence prevail in you for 24 hours and then sit down in a corner of your house and write down your own experience of 24 hours silence. You will experience innumerable miracles happening in your own life just by having a 24 hours complete silence of thoughts. You will experience even solutions to various problems for which you have not been able to get the answer for quite long. Hence, it is time now for you at least to think of 24 hours silence of thought programme or a Maun. To achieve the best results start at least once a year and then try to do once a month and see the miracle of the benefits you get by adopting this simple programme. I am happy to share with the readers that couple of years ago once I had experienced the magic and the miracle of silence of thoughts for 24 hours I had planned to take a group of my friends, relatives and the members of Investors Club of which I am the Secretary General and we organized all the group comprising of more than 100 people to experience of magic of silence of thoughts. We went all the way from Delhi to the Ashram of Brahmakumari and there all participants young and old jointly practiced the concept of silence of thoughts. Initially it was a problem as to how to keep silence for 24 hours and more particularly for the ladies it was too difficult. But at the end of the day, all the participants who went, maintained complete silence for 24 hours and each one had a wonderful experience to share with the other person. I want all the readers and their families to experience this wonderful magic of silence. If you find that you are not able to experience this magic individually, then do get in touch with me on my E-Mail – slakhotia@satyam.net.in and write to me that you are interested in the programme of 24 hours silence. As and when the next programme is finalized, I will keep you informed and it will be our pleasure if you join us. Super success comes nearer to you with the practice of silence.

56

Listen carefully & reply with nodding

Listen carefully to others. Make your personality, a personality of the real hero, a personality which can be classified as a super successful person. Hence, develop this habit of listening carefully and "Nodding your head" when you are talking to someone. It will indicate that you are listening and you care for the thoughts of the other person.

57

Mortgage your house for super success

Those who want to make big money and feel that super success is to be measured only in terms of monetary value, then to them the mantra is mortgage your house for super success and go on paying interest but work hard and use the money from mortgage to run big business, more business and thus more money and more success.

58

Put your extra hours to work even without over time payment

Your boss will pay you overtime for your work and you work. This is nothing great. Every person in the world will work for the overtime getting extra payment. But the point is that a super successful person works even without overtime. Try and try this concept once at least and then you see the advantage which you get in the long term. It is time now for you to work some extra hours may be even without pay but this type of working overtime without being paid brings you more closer to your boss, gives the stamp of your commitment to the organization and this activity helps you to come more closer to your immediate boss and then the road is there which leads you to super success.

59

Your Fitness Formula for Super Success

Physical fitness at every point of the day is a must for all those who are on the road to achieve super success. You can resort to the concepts like spiritual healing and the concepts like regular pranayam, yoga and meditation. All these activities will help you to remain fit whole of the day and thus, your road to super success becomes a little bit more easy.

60

Develop curiosity for your super success

Always be curious about new activities, new ideas, new vistas and thrill of the future success of yours. Curiosity once stopped, then your super success receives a back gear in life. Hence, never let curiosity stopped. Be inquisite and be curious about all new ideas, visions, vistas etc. then super success will be near to you.

61

Liberal appreciation to one and all

It is the quality of a super successful person to appreciate one and all whether it is the home front, whether it is the office front or whether it is the relative's front or your social front. Let you develop inbuilt quality of extending liberal appreciation to one and all whom you meet. The biggest advantage of extending liberal appreciation is that your inner self does not become dark and that you are vibrant as usual. There is no loss to you by extending appreciation and you get only better love and affection from all those who come near you.

62

Start to finish, finish to start

Make it a habit to start your activity and finish to start some activity which you want to start. Well, start in time. Don't just ponder and ponder but only start. And once you start, just aim to finish the work in time. Do not keep many items pending and scattered. More the items kept pending, more will be the anxiety and tension. For a super successful person, the theme should be 'start to finish and finish to start' something new.

63

Always think of providing happiness to one and all

Whether someone provides you happiness or not but your aim in life should be to provide happiness to one and all whom you meet in your life. Hence, make it a point that you would always extend happiness to all the persons who come in contact with you. A super successful person is also very popular–popular amongst relatives, popular amongst friends and popular amongst colleagues and business associates. The simple reason of your popularity is that you should go on extending happiness to all whom you meet, then surely your happiness will be doubled. Most of the times, providing happiness costs nothing and thus without incurring any expenditure you can extend small courtesies in life which may provide happiness to others. For example, I find that many times during the year I get invitations to attend marriage functions and parties from my fans who watch my regular TV show. I have no relationship with them. But if I can make it up, I try to visit sometimes their functions, programmes, marriage ceremony and other activities in their life which make them happy and provide bliss and happiness to them, unlimited. By seeing their happiness I become double happy. Hence, always think of providing happiness to one and all.

64

Super success for persons making 28 hours a day

Well, you may say that in the whole world all persons whether rich or poor, whether intellectual or otherwise, have a 24 hour day only. In that case what are we talking about 28 hours a day! Yes, it is true. You can also make 28 hours a day. More particularly for all those persons who want to achieve super success in life making 28 hours a day is a must. Well, the simple formula is to ensure that you do not waste any time in your 24 a day and also add a couple of hours which otherwise would have been wasted to your list and thereby make 28 hours of your day. I remember my father R.N. Lakhotia who happens to be India's leading Tax Authority and who had a very struggling life up to the period when he was a student. As my grandmother had died while my father was in his teens, he had to take care of the household work also including fetching water from the local tap. Yes, in those times this was the system and one had to waste lot of time standing in the queue to get water from the tap. At that time my father while standing in the queue would keep a copy in his hand and would revise the new words every day. This is one example of how you can make 28 hours in a day. Similarly, while we were in Kolkata 25 years ago and myself and my Daddy used to appear in Income-tax cases of our clients and there was a long wait outside the Office of the Income-tax Officer. We could see most of the tax consultants and the chartered accountants while sitting and waiting for their turn to come in, they would either gossip or have a cup of tea. But I would see my father waiting outside the Office of the Income-tax Officer and correcting some proofs of the books or writing an article or correcting the matter typed by the steno. These live examples of my father have helped me in my life to make my 28 hours a day by taking advantage of cutting down on the wastage of the time and utilizing the time always. Even nowadays while I travel a lot for my seminars in different parts of India, I try to ensure that each day I make 28 hours a day hence, right from the time when I enter the airport I am busy. Once the security is over, I am on my job either to do an evening walk in the waiting lounge of the airport or to sit down and correct some article or to think about some matter etc. Hence, do agree that it is possible for everyone to make 28 hours a day and also please note that your making 28 hours in a day will place you an added advantage in comparison with your colleagues. After all there must be some difference between the super successful person and the normal person. Try to aim that you have to certainty make 28 hours in a day. Only then you can have super success and you will definitely be able to make it.

65

Free from the clutches of fear

Patanjali Yogasutra says that one should never be fearful. Hence, it is time now for you to shed your fear at every point of time in life. Please remember that what is needed is an action plan and not just fear. Fear will take away your creativity and would put you in the back gear. As against that your fearlessness will bring more creativity in you and will bring out the best in you.

66

Listen to your inner soul

Yes, sit down in a calm and quiet place and start listening to your inner soul. Do remember that if you are able to listen to your inner soul, you are able to find answers to those complicated problems of your life and also to the problems of better living in this mysterious world. Hence, always take out some time to listen to the top show going on inside your soul and do have faith on what the soul says.

67

Happiness unlimited

Let happiness be a part of your joyful life. A super successful person is happy always round the clock in all circumstances. Hence, be happy. Only then you can achieve super success.

68

Blame none for your failures

Generally people are in the habit of blaming others for all the failures that has happened to the project or to them or in some activity of life. However, the super successful person thinks of the solutions and does not merely think about the failures in life. He does not aim at accusing his colleague or friend or business associate. Hence, develop the habit of accuse none rather praise them more.

69

Live not today but live this time

At this moment you should live wonderfully well and enjoy this moment of life which has been made available to you by the courtesy that came to you by the Almighty God. Think like this always. On the top of your mind always think of not the past, not the future, not even today but this time. Then only you are a super successful person.

70

Positive Commitment

Whether it is business commitments or your service related commitments or commitments towards your family and the relatives, let all your commitments in life be positive commitments. A positive committed person makes others imbibe positiveness and thus he becomes a super successful person.

71

Inspire, Inform, Involve – One and all

The super successful person has the inherent qualities to inspire his colleagues and business associates and also to inform the new technology, the way of doing some activity to all persons around him and finally it is this super successful person who involves everyone connected with him in his activity to produce the best results in whatever he is doing.

72

Never worry about what has not happened

I have seen many persons in life who have ruined their career in service as well as in business merely because these persons were worrying about the uncertain future. Future is uncertain and it is true. But what is in your hand is not to worry about all those uncertainties in the life which have not happened at all. Hence, do not worry at all about all that which has not happened. I have seen some of the people getting worried by seeing the fall in the sensex. While some people get worried when they find that the international exports from India has dropped and they fear that their exports turnover may also be decreased. While some persons get worried just thinking that their CEO would leave their organization. Thousands and may be more are the pointers about which you can think and think and get worried for all that which has not yet happened. But it is the super successful person who never becomes worried about anything which has not happened.

73

Don't be hopeless

I have gone through some difficult times – who hasn't ? – and I know how easy it is to think that troubles have become your constant companions. Yet let a gray film of hopelessness creep into your mind, where it colors everything. You can even begin to enjoy this sense of hopelessness. It gives you an excuse for not trying to improve the situation! This is what Norman Vincen Peale used to say. Finally while talking about hope, Peale feels that the remedy for this state of mind is a good strong dose of hope, given to yourself at least three times a day. Don't ever say to yourself I have had it, I am finished, I can't cope with all this. Never think, this is more than I can take, it is more than I can handle. Well, these inspiring words of Peale would really inspire all the readers to never think of hopelessness in life.

74

Breakfast, lunch and dinner with hope salad

I have been inspired by Norman Vincen Peale and his writings have talked about hope which actually represents your ability to fight your way through the series of discouragement and depression. Peale feels that it is this little four letter word "hope" that has enormous powers in it. Hope has the power to bring the weak back to strength and all this power is in hope alone. Martin Luther used to say that everything that is done in the world is done by hope. Hence, have a wonderful breakfast, lunch and dinner with the hope salad as a part of your day to day activity. Only then you can become a super successful person.

75

It is time to melt down the fear of the unknown

The fear of the unknown is very successful in taking away and eating away all your energy and creativity. Hence, never let the fear of the unknown overpower your think tank in your mind.

76

Super successful person makes 14 days in a week

We all are aware that a week has just 7 days. But what I am talking is not for a normal person. But for a super successful person, a week comprises 14 days but not 7 days. It sounds absurd but it is true. I also attempt to make 14 days in a week and all my readers can also make their week of 14 days. Well, if you are interested to make your week of 14 days, then just follow the simple formula. On a piece of paper write down all the days of the week starting from Monday until Sunday. Now in each day keep two partitions, the morning day and the evening day. Divide your day in two parts starting from 6 A.M. to 2 P.M. and second half of the day starting from 2 P.M. until 10 P.M. Once you have divided each day of the week in two parts namely the morning day and the evening day, then you find that for your 7 days in a week, each day you are having the morning day as well as the evening day and thus for 7 days in a week. The total number of days available at your control is 14. Write down on a piece of paper the chart of two days of every day of the week and in this 14 day chart in which you should write down important activities which you propose to do. Once you follow this chart and vigorously pursue this chart on daily basis, then surely you will find that your week comprises of total 14 days and that your creativity has improved and many things which you thought you will not be able to do now you have made it possible for doing it and this is really the miracle of your 14 day in a week.

77

Double look before you leap

'Look before you leap' is the dictum we have learnt long back while we were in the school. However, the latest dictum for all those who would like to achieve super success is the dictum known as "Double Look Before you Leap". Yes, it is true that whenever you leap, you must make sure rather doubly make sure that what you are stating for is correct. This is a simple statement but definitely a very very important one. To give you a classic example I would like to narrate the actual incident which happened with me . The other day I was traveling with a friend of mine from NOIDA to Delhi. My friend's son who has just completed his MBA was also in the car. We were having a general chat about the real estate business activities. My friend is into real estate sector and is investing heavily with different builders in NOIDA, Gurgaon and in other parts of NCR. I was listening to the conversation between my friend and his son. They were talking about the total number of partnership firms which had invested their money with one builder. My friend said that with that specific builder four of his partnership firms had made investments in the real estate projects of the said developer in NOIDA. His son immediately reacted to this answer and said no daddy, no, there were minimum five partnership firms in which we have made investments with a builder. My friend was very confident that there were only four firms with whom they had made the said investment and that his firmness was based on the builderwise investment chart which he has prepared the same day in the morning. My friend's son said okay then let us have a bet whether you are right or I am right. Very confident from his face my friend happily agreed and said okay let us have a bet and the father son had a bet of Rs.1000. The deal was if it is proved that there were five firms, then obviously the father would pay Rs.1000 to the son but reversely if it was proved that there were only four firms with whom they had investments, then definitely the son would pay Rs.1000 to his father. I was surprised with this type of conversation between father and son because I am not accustomed to this type of betting between father and son. But I feel that this is the way of life and this is the way the children live these days with their parents as they are very much informal more particularly if you find that your children are foreign educated, they definitely become very informal with their parents. Gone are the days of keeping distance between father and son to have a dialogue. Anyway, now to make sure that the son was very serious, he immediately took out two notes of Rs.500 each and put it in his father's hand. Father's face was with cheers and the great satisfaction it could be seen on his face as he was sure that he would now today win the bet from his foreign educated son. Obviously the confidence of the father was mainly because of the chart which he has himself prepared couple of hours ago on the same day and it was crystal clear in his mind that there were only four firms with whom they had invested with the builder and now while the car was still proceeding and was very near to their residence, the son said to his father okay Dad if I lose, I will pay you Rs.1000 and have given you in advance Rs.1000 to show my bonafide and intention that I am really serious. But if you lose, then you are to pay me Rs.3000. Dad very casually agreed because he was so very confident that he cannot be wrong. And now the car stopped just outside their house. We all entered the drawing room. I could see the face of my friend very bright and confident that he would now win the bet and this was reflected from his face but equally when I saw the face of the son, I found him too confident. His face was also bubbling with enthusiasm. He was hoping to win a bet of Rs.3000 from his father. Now my friend immediately rushed to his chamber and took out the files and papers which he had prepared in the morning and checked the papers. The paper was in his hand and it showed 1, 2, 3, 4 i.e. total four firms of his group which had invested with a builder and now his face again showed the signs of great victory he had achieved as if he has won some big war because he has won the bet from his MBA and foreign returned son. The son highly qualified young man educated from abroad and recently back to India said to his Dad. Okay Dad, you have seen the list which said that you had invested with four firms only. But let us have a look at all those partnership firms which we have got in our group to find out if you had left by chance any firm in the list prepared by you. My friend in any case was very much confident that today he is going to win the bet and more particularly when he had prepared the list himself early morning on the same day. Now came the time to finally decide who the winner was of this bet. My friend now started seeing all the files, papers and documents to re-prepare the chart of the firms who had invested with the builder. When he had concluded preparing the chart, he was shocked to find that it was not four but five firms who had invested with the said builder and now his smiling face turned out to be a dark face because he had lost the bet from his son. Coolly in slow motion his hands went into his pocket and he took out three notes of each of Rs.1000 and gave it to his son because he had lost the bet against his son. This real story would convince all the readers that it is always better to double look before you leap.

Always prepare your papers and documents carefully and before taking any decision based on such papers or documents, you must always double check the contents etc. of such papers or documents so that you do not cut a sorry figure. All those who are going to be super successful persons in their life, should make it a point that they should always double check any facts or papers or statements before taking a final decision based on such papers so that no embarrassment and no financial loss would occur to them. This is an important mantra for super successful persons.

78

Did you thank God today?

You are successful, no you are super successful and you feel very proud for your achievement. Well, it is good to be super successful but the point is that you should never stop thanking the Almighty God with whose grace success has been showered on you. Everyday think a while on the single point namely "Did you thank God today?" In my colony every morning when I walk through the lanes of my colony for going to the park for a morning walk outside one building I see a play card which states the caption "Did you thank God today?" The first time when I saw this play card, for a moment I just stopped outside this building and read the play card two, three, five and ten times and now the slogan mentioned on the play card is in my heart and everyday before I retire, I always try to answer the question posted on the play card namely did I thank God today. Make it a habit everyday to thank the Almighty. A thought of this type will bring great strength for you and would bring super success for you.

79

Formula WAP in case of crisis

For a pretty successful person crisis would be part of the game. The point is when you are surrounded by unprecedented crisis in all the four corners of your life, then the question arises what do you do. Managing the crisis at its peak is one of the salient features of a real superb successful person and I am confident that formula WAP is the sure answer for your crisis management. Hence, at any point of time in your life if you come across crisis facing you in business, in industry, in life, then just adopt the formula WAP. This formula WAP has been prepared by me and has been successfully implemented by lakhs of people throughout the world for managing their crisis. Well now the question comes after all what is formula WAP is? Formula WAP means *Work Action Plan.* This formula WAP (Work Action Plan) implies that whenever you are in the crisis and you find that crisis are there on all the fronts of your personality, then at that point of time just adopt the concept of Work Action Plan and then you find that your crisis run away very fast. With WAP your crisis are out from your agenda. I remember one leading builder of New Delhi was facing acute financial problem. He was facing crisis in all fronts of his business. He was unable to make payment schedule for his suppliers and so also he was unable to fulfill the payment schedules of the bank and finally from the lenders also he was facing great crisis because he was unable to make their payment commitment. Well, at such a point of time when he was facing all different problems in his business, he was in a fix as to how to handle such crisis coming not from one front but crisis coming from each and every corner of his office. When I met him I asked him to adopt and implement in action the concept of WAP – that is Work Action Plan. A 90 minutes brain storming with this builder made him feel strong and face the crisis in his business. He immediately adopted Work Action Plan and then started working in the right direction. Crisis was there, problems were there, financial constraints were there but then all these have to be handled by proper application of the mind and working and working and working. I told him to jot down all his problems daily and thereafter we started preparing the Work Action Plan. Just in one month the Work Action Plan that is formula WAP made him come out from his crisis management and he was now a wonderful person once again away from different crisis of his business.

80

One plus one is not two, not 11 but it is 111

Super successful persons in business and industry in particular value the concept of one plus one. Please note that if you are in business or industry and some friends or relatives join you in business, then you are not one plus one is equal to two. Sometimes people think that if in business or industry, we unite one plus one, then we become eleven. But my experience of life is one plus one is never two nor it is eleven but the fact remains that one plus one becomes 111. Have faith in this concept. Have regard, love and respect for this concept and finally sit down to venture into that business activity where you will combine with someone else and then make it 111.

81

Live in the realities of life

All those who are super successful persons should live in this world based on the realities of the life. One cannot live in the unreal world. Hence, if you adopt the concept of living in the realities of the life, then you find that you are really a super successful person.

82

Confess to yourself

Have the guts and the ability to confess. The virtue of confessing makes you great. The habit of confessing makes you honourable in the presence of your friends or business associates. Hence, if you commit a mistake or if you are wrong somewhere then it is no point eyeing and justifying your point of view but better course is to confess. Confession makes your heart light. It brings out unnecessary tension from your mind. Hence, always develop the habit of confessing to yourself.

83

Let smile be part of your daily life

'Smile and the world smiles with you. Weep and you weep alone.' Well this is a dictum which is time tested but let me tell you that the present studies made by a University in USA states that if you smile, then your life span increases. Hence, if you continue to adopt the concept of smiling all the way all the time, then you are able to increase your life span near about seven years. Every super successful person would surely like to increase his life span. Hence, smiling is one of the wonderful ways to increase your life span.

84

Realise the heaven within you

Super successful person virtually lives in the heaven. Well, heaven you may say we have not seen. Well, the heaven which we are talking is within yourself. Hence, it is time now to realize this heaven. I remember the following saying of Swami Ram Tirth which is a fact for a super successful person :-

Realise the heaven within you, and all at once all the desires are fulfilled all the misery and suffering is put an end to.

Lo! The trees of the wood are my next of kin.
And the rocks alive with what beats in me.
The clay is my flesh, and the fox my skin.
I am fierce with gadfly and sweet with the bee.
The flower is naught but the bloom of my love.
And the waters run down in the tune I dream.
The sun is my flower, up hung above.
I cannot die, though forever death.
Weave back and fro in the warp of me.
I was never born, yet my births of breath.
Are as many as waves on the sleepless sea,
Oh, Heaven is within you, seek Happiness not in
The objects of sense; realize that Happiness is with yourself.

85

Always avoid AFA

A famous magazine in its lead article wrote that stress, frustration and aggression are common problems of people who have fragile emotional support systems which can be a common occurrence in today's pressure cooker existence. They can cause physical and emotional problems that may seriously damage health. The bad news in these psychological problems can grow at a rapid pace. Studies show that the manifestation of tension, anger and social belligerence include tense muscles, headaches and insomnia. Depression and irritability are the products. They may hinder your concentration and memory besides putting you at risk of heart attack and stroke. But the good news is that you can learn to avoid your "stress-building" thoughts and replace them with the positive "stress bursting" ones.

Well, the fact remains that in this machine–age, anger, frustration as well as aggression are common to most of the people. But please do remember that your anger, your frustration and your aggression bring no advantage to you but it only brings disadvantages for your robust health and for your personality. Hence, if you want to be a super successful person, always avoid anger, frustration and aggression (AFA). Pranayam twice in a day for five minutes will help you in overcoming anger and frustration. Giving positive suggestions to yourself coming direct from your soul and mind will also help you to avoid anger, frustration and aggression(AFA).

86

This too shall pass

If you are super successful in any field, in any walk of life, then great problems, tensions, worries and other related problems will be faced by you on daily basis. However, you should have faith in the dictum of the God namely 'this too shall pass away'. Hence, whenever you are in trouble, always have great faith on the slogan – 'This too shall pass away'. I recollect a wonderful story which was printed in Times of India in their supplement on the occasion of Woman`s Day Special. This story has been told by Rajashree Birla, the Chairperson of Aditya Birla Centre for Community Initiatives and Rural Development. The story is as follows:

Once upon a time, there lived this Jewish king named Solomon. In a grumpy mood, he thought of teaching Benamiah Ben Yehoyada, his minister, a lesson. So he assigned to him a seemingly impossible task. He ordered Benamiah to find him a magic ring with extraordinary features. And that was - if you were joyous and wore it, you would feel absolutely sad!

Solomon gave him a six-month timeline for the search. Deep down in their hearts, both Solomon and Benamiah knew that such a ring did not exist in this universe. Benamiah prayed hard for a miracle. A little before the deadline was over, and having walked all over for a such a ring, he decided to go to one of the poorest places in Jerusalem.

There was an old merchant who was spreading out his goods on a carpet. Benamiah was quite intrigued. He thought, "Let me take chance with him." Therefore, he asked the merchant whether he had a magic ring that could make a happy person forget his happiness and sad person forget his sorrows. The merchant smiled. He took a gold ring from his wares and etched four words on it. Benamiah took the gold ring. When he read the inscription he was extremely happy. He felt that his mission was accomplished. He went back to Solomon. Solomon and all his ministers began making a mockery of Benamiah, teasing him as he would have returned empty-handed. Benamiah smiled and offered the gold ring to His Majesty. As soon as Solomon read what was written, he stopped being a tease. The words were "This too shall pass" . Suddenly, Solomon felt that everything in life was ephemeral, and nothing lasts forever.

These four words – 'This too shall pass' – have always given me tremendous strength, resilience and a lot of hope. Subsequently, I learnt that the phrase gained global fame when Abraham Lincoin, the former US President, used it in one of his speeches.

A little aside, I believe that if you view life through the lens of a positive prism, you will only be greeted with positivity.

I think the above mentioned simple but important message conveyed in the story by Rajashree Birla would continue to give strength to all those persons who want to achieve super success in their life. I can say from my own experience that this four word message of - "This too shall pass" will give us strength at times when we are faced with great and grave problems in life. Only point is we should have faith in this dictum.

87

Stress free lifestyle

Super successful person would always have a stress free life style. If you are not able to control your stress, then what type of super successful person you are. Recently Rohit Bal, 42, a leading fashion designer, suffered a massive heart attack and it is a warning bell for all those persons who are leading a highly stressed life style. Hence, super successful person should never keep stress on his neck. Rather if you want to keep stress, keep it below your leg. Stress free life maintained would provide bliss, peace and happiness and would help a person to go further in the wonderland of achieving super success.

88

Become what you want to be

Super successful person should always think that if they have faith, they can do what they like. It is my recommendation to all those persons who would like to achieve super success that they should do what they would like to do. Hence, the bliss of life comes when you are able to do what you would like to do. For the young my message is–become what you want to be and you would become. What all is needed is complete dedication, devotion and a single goal which alone will make you what you really want to be. I remember Dilip Chhabaria, one of India's topmost automobile designer, when he was a child, his time was spent mostly in sketching cars. His fascination for cars led him to the Automotive Art School at Pasadena in United States of America. After completing his art course in the world famous Automotive Art School he served for a short period at General Motors and returned to India. In 1993 when he started his activity, his company had merely eight employees on his payrolls. But Chhabaria now has 400 people working for him and he turns more than 250 unique cars in a year. Now Chhabaria is interested to diversify into designing furniture, refrigerator and television. So what you want to be you will be. Have faith in the dictum and just proceed with complete dedication to your theme goal. I would like to also share with you a small story which I read recently in the Yogakshema magazine and which inspired me. Here is the story :- Let me tell about a little girl who was born into a very poor family in a shack in the Backwoods of Tennessee.

She was the 20th of 22 children, prematurely born and frail. Her survival was doubtful. When she was four years old, she had double pneumonia and scarlet fever - a deadly combination that left her with a paralyzed and useless left leg. She had to wear an iron leg brace. Yet, she was fortunate in having a mother who encouraged her.

Well, this mother told her little girl, who was very bright, that despite the brace and leg, she could do whatever she wanted to do with her life. She told here that all she needed to do was to have faith, persistence, courage and indomitable spirit.

So at nine years of age, the little girl removed the leg brace, and she took the step. The doctors told her she would never walk normally. In four years, she developed a rhythmic stride, which was a medical wonder. Then this girl got the notion, the incredible notion, that she would like to be the world's greatest woman runner. Now, what could she mean – be a runner with leg like that?

At the age 13, she entered a race. She came in last – way, way last. She entered every race in high school, and in every race she came last. Everyone begged her quit! However, one day, she came in next to last. And then there came a day when she won a race. From then on, Wilma Rudolph won every race that she entered.

Wilma went to Tennessee State University, where she met a coach name Ed Temple. Coach Temple saw the indomitable spirit of the girl, that she was a believer and that she had great natural talent. He trained her so well that she went to the Olympic Games.

There she was pitted against the greatest woman runner of the day, a German girl named Jutta Heine. Nobody had ever beaten Jutta. But in the 100-meter race, Wilma Rudolph won. She beat Jutta again in the 200-meters. Now Wilma had two Olympic gold medals.

Finally came the 400-meter relay, it would be Wilma against Jutta again. The first two runners on Wilma's team made perfect handoffs with the baton. But when the third runner handed the baton to Wilma, she was so excited she dropped it, and Wilma saw Jutta taking off down the track. It was impossible that any body could catch this fleet and nimble girl. But, Wilma did just that! Wilma Rudolph had earned three Olympic gold medals.

This small actual life story would surely inspire each and every one to dream to do what you would like to do.

89

Change destiny with your desire

If you desire, you can definitely change your destiny by hard work and super dedication. In the past, inspired by this theme alone a large number of successful persons throughout the world have changed their destiny just because of their keen desire to change it. To get the inspiration on this theme please read the wonderful message given on this point in the Brihadaranyaka Upanishad where it is stated that : You are what your deep driving desire is; as your desire is; so your will is; as your will is; so your deed is; as your deed is; so your destiny is. Thus, it is possible for you to change your destiny with your keen desire and action plan. One should definitely have faith in oneself and the ability to achieve the goals should be the desire. I remember the wonderful words of Henry Ford who said whether you believe you can or whether you believe you cannot you are right. Thus, try to achieve the impossible. Try to change the destiny. Try to change the astrological fate of yours only by your desire and hard work. It is better that you place on the mirror in your bathroom the following words :

I am looking at the face of the person who is going to be responsible for my success and for my super success today. Repeat : I am looking at the face of the person who is going to be responsible for my super success.

90

Always with an entrepreneurship dream

Dream and dream. Dream for becoming a successful entrepreneur and be after your dream strongly confirm to yourself that you will definitely achieve super success in your life. I was influenced by a very good passage printed in one of the old issues of *Yogakshema* wherein it was written that when we were young, we had dreams and expectations. We imagine things, we keep thinking about what we want to be, what we want to do, what makes us proud and happy and what will become.

We grew up, and things seemed like having its own way. We accept our success or failures and we move on. The rapid change, the need to do the urgent things, the works, the pressures and the failures, all kill part of our visions. Things have changed, but they cannot really take away the dreams. We will have to dream on, to visualize our desires, our wants, our vision of our future, even when we are considered too old for such things.

Cornel Sanders started his business when he was 60, and started the whole successful KFC business. The main thing is not the age – whether being too old, or too young, but it is desire to dream on, and the courage to realize it. Vivid visualization, taking it to sleep, thinking constantly about it, talking about it, planning it adding all the spices to our dreams will make us a bit closer to the realization of our dreams.

Entrepreneurship starts with a dream, a simple wish of tiny restaurant operation, or a huge business of real estate development, or a modest training centre for English education, or just any other self-employed money earning fun.

The ability to dream on is one of the fine quality of human race that other species do not posses. So dream on, and put a deadline. Make it a giant dream, a tiny one, an old everlasting one, a newfound one, a hobby related one, a change of life one, a religious one, a stupid one, a stroke-of-genius one, or just whatever... just continue to dream on... Then, just Go and Do it !

91

Double love your employees

A super successful person cannot achieve the super success just because of him alone. It is your employees who are equally the driving force to make your rise and make your prosperity in the worldly sense. Hence, it is time for you now not merely to love your employees but to double love your employees. Develop this art and this art will definitely repay great risk awards and rewards for you in your business. The other day I met one General Manager, Corporate Affairs working in a big Real Estate Development Company. He narrated one interesting incident which happened to him. Although he had joined the company in less than a year ago, one fine morning when he entered his office, his boss, the Managing Director summoned him to his cabin. This General Manager of Corporate Affairs was unable to understand as to why the Managing Director of the company invited him. Generally, the General Manager would report to the Senior Vice President and very rarely he would have an occasion to meet the Chairman of the company. Anyway he entered the cabin of his Chairman and then he was merely surprised to find that his Chairman presented him a very big bouquet of flowers because the day happened to be the birthday of General Manager, Corporate Affairs. This small activity by the Chairman of the company towards the Senior Manager shows the warmth of love and affection for the employees and also reflect the character of the person with regard to the message that we care for you, Hence, not just love but extend double love to your employees and then you find that your employees are dedicated to you in a true sense.

92

Develop your Will Power

Every super successful person should aim at development of his Will Power. Swami Sivanand used to lay great emphasis on development of the Will Power. According to him, Will Power is the ability to control one's own movements and internal states, feelings and thoughts by conscious and deliberate choice. It is the faculty or power of the mind by which we determine either to do or not to do something.

Patience and perseverance, application and tenacity, overcoming dislikes and irritations, controlling the temper, keeping a daily diary - all pave a long way to developing the will. Try and hear the words of others patiently even though they are not interesting or charming. Do not fret and fume.

Doing actions or tasks that are uninteresting also develops the will power. Anywhere you go there will be difficulties. Never complain about your environment. Try to live happily in any place, under any condition. You will become strong, dynamic and successful in any undertaking. You will be able to conquer any difficulty. One who has a firm, strong will power can accomplish anything. So when you have to achieve super success then you have to develop will power.

93

Imbibe principles in life

A super successful person should imbibe the famous principles of life to make life a really wonderful and super successful personality in you. Well, these 18 principles have been prescribed by Swami Sivanand who used to have great faith in these 18 principles which according to him would make a perfect man. These 18 principles promulgated by Swami Sivanand are : serenity, regularity, absence of vanity, sincerity, simplicity, veracity, equanimity, fixity, non-irritability, adaptability, humility, tenacity, integrity, nobility, magnanimity, charity, generosity and purity.

Swami Sivananda has given very clear indications on the yogic principles that one should try to imbibe in life. As a teacher, for one month practice serenity for ten minutes before your class, and then give the class, maintaining that state of serenity. As a yoga teacher, for one month, practice absence of vanity. First, observe your vanity, then try to control your reactions, your ego, your pride and give the class, observing yourself, as well as the students.

Swami Sivananda is of the view that yoga teachers should become more humble students because along with teaching in the class, they should be learning to manage themselves. When we have the idea of teaching, we identify with the ego. When there is ego identification, then connecting with yogic principles is not possible. Telling people how to practice yoga or how to teach yoga is not really the criterion of a yoga teacher. In order to excel as a yoga teacher, after the training you have to identify with the principles of yoga rather than with the practices. Teach people the practices of yoga, but you yourself should practice the principles of yoga. Only by training yourself in how to manage your own mental agitation and negativity can you become a good yoga teacher.

If you aim to imbibe the above mentioned 18 principles of life and if you are able to implement at least 10 principles in life, then you are a successful person. But if you are able to achieve 15 plus from the above mentioned list of 18 principles, then surely you are a super successful person.

94

Maintain your self-esteem

Maintaining or developing self esteem is good. Yoga which happens to be the art and science of living in harmony with the nature teaches you the principles and practice of self-esteem. Self esteem means feeling good about oneself. If you develop the habit of self esteem and if you maintain your self esteem thinking that yes you are a wonderful person, a worthwhile person in the community village in regardless of what people may say or they may not say, then it is your own self esteem which will help you in doing away with inferiority complex, if any. The fact remains that we all use only 10 per cent of our brain potential and 90 per cent of the brain potential is actually not used by us but if we respect our own self esteem, then surely we will be able to have a better personality in ourselves. The fault lies in faulty planning of our own mind and not caring about the self esteem. Hence, start caring for your own self esteem and try to continue to maintain your self esteem.

95

Adopt Swan principles

A super successful person should take inspiration from Swan. Hence, adopting Swan principles will help you achieve great success in your life. Swami Sivamurti Saraswati has very nicely analysed the Swan principles. According to him the Swan principles can help us achieve a lot. It is also necessary to accept the present realities of life that relate to our bodies and minds. Do you accept your body? You may want to be slim, but you are naturally chubby. You have to accept that. Then you can bring about change. Acceptance does not necessarily mean agreement. We learn to discern which qualities about ourselves we need to accept and which ones we need to change.

The SWAN principle can help us achieve more control over our lives. Symbolically, the swan, *hamsa* in Sanskrit, means one who can discriminate, one who can separate true from false, one who can see beyond appearances and read between the lines, and one who has right understanding. The SWAN technique teaches us to recognize and to know our strengths, weaknesses, ambitions and needs, and to learn to accept them. It is quite easy to accept our strengths, but it may not be so easy to accept our weaknesses because we don't want them and we feel vulnerable with them. Swami Satyananada has said that only great men and women know their limitations. Therefore, it is very important to know not only our strengths but also our weaknesses, so that we can accept them and begin to work on ourselves to transform them into strengths.

We also need to know what our ambitions are. We need long term and short term aims. For example, a long term aim might be to experience self-realization. That's not necessarily going to happen today or tomorrow. We may need it as a long term aim and it may give our life meaning, but we also need short term aims that we can achieve easily. This can give us a certain satisfaction, self-esteem and confidence that we managed to do what we set out to do. Making a list of your ambitions will bring a new awareness and way of looking at things in your mind.

96

Learn to excel, excel to serve

At every point of time try to make the habit that you keep your focus always on excelling others in all walks of life. If you think that I have achieved already the story of success and there is nothing to excel anyone in the world, then that day stops your journey in super success arena. Not merely excel others but what is needed is after excelling others it is time now to serve the community, serve the brothers and sisters, serve all those who come in contact with you.

97

Don't worry just act

One need not worry at all in adversity. Here is an example: two shops next to each other continue business. One shop owner puts a big sign board outside his shop to say "Big Sale". The second shop owner immediately put's a signboard outside the shop which says "Huge Discount". Now the first shop owner got desperate when he found that next day with the caption huge discount the customers were going to the next door shop only resulting into meager sale for his products. He was a super successful person. He thought of a strategy for the shop. The placard which read Big Sale, he removed the placard and then he put a new placard which just read Main Entrance. You will be surprised but the fact is just by changing the placard with the caption Main Entrance, the next day unprecedented crowd came to his shop. The passer by saw the sign board on the second shop which said Huge Discount but when to the first shop because there was a placard which said Main Entrance. Hence, whenever there is a point to worry in business, in life etc., do not worry. But at that point of time just think and take an important management decision how to overcome the worry.

98

Do something which puts a smile on the face of others

A super successful person does not look only at the horizons of his own personality development but goes a step forward and tries to think of vision, vistas and ideas which aims at putting a smile on the face of others. Do maintain always in mind the concept of give and take. You have already taken from the society so much that has been instrumental to make you the real you and the real super successful person. Hence, it is time now for you to give back to the society. Very few corporate enterprises although earning lakhs and crores but the mindset is not for going in for those activities which would provide a smile on the face of others. So, if you want to receive a bliss of life and enjoy the real happiness, it is time for you now to think and remember to give something that you enjoy yourself and that something to be given to those who cannot afford it. Your giving something will bring smile on the face of others. It is not big money. What is needed is the thought process of your mind. Hence, whether you are a rich person or a middle class person, take time now to the concept of life thinking after achieving your super success aim at providing a smile on the face of others.

99

Enjoy family life and holiday

A super successful person always aims at being super successful in all Walks of life and to have a holistic experience of achieving super success. One of the vistas is to enjoy family life and the holiday with the family. In the film industry there are 100 top film personalities who have had a big success in life but there are very few who have made a holistic super success. One such person is the leading film star of Bollywood industry namely Akshay Kumar. Commenting about family life and holiday Akshay Kumar can be said to be one of the finest persons in the Bollywood industry who is a super successful person and also enjoys the family life and holiday. Commenting on family life and holiday in one of the interviews recently Akshay Kumar said " I have a very simple life with my wife. I attend only 2-3 parties a year. I lead a very secluded life completely away from the industry. Twinkle and I are in bed by 9-30 p.m. We go alone on holidays with our son. Every 3-4 months we take a week off and every year we take full month off. I put a globe in front of my wife and son, and tell them to pick wherever they choose to go. Last year, we went to New York, Barbados and Puerto Rico", says Akshay Kumar.

100

Use to adopt 13D Formula

There is no short cut to success. This is a fact and specially when you want to achieve not success but super success, then never think of any short cut to your road of super success. It is only due to continued hard work, dedication and devotion to your activities of life which alone will be responsible to make you a super successful person. However, the super successful youth in particular should adopt the 13D Formula for super success. These items of 13D are : dedication, devotion, discipline, determination, detachment, development, decision, deepness, divinity, design, desire, desist, dictum.

101

The Power of Determination

The fact remains that a super successful person always has to be different from others and one important point on which the difference would lie between a super successful and a non-super successful person is the power of determination. A super successful person would always have greater ever power of determination. It is his this spirit of determination which alone would make him the real king in the wonderland of super success. I remember one interesting and inspiring story with regard to the power of determination. This is a story about Abraham Lincoln, the former President of USA. It was a time when Abraham Lincoln was living a very dreadful life. He was not able to make his both ends meet. He was unable to get food for two times in a day. Still in spite of the adverse situation he would not think, he would not be baffled and would not accept the defeat in life. He was taking great interest in reading but he was unable to purchase books. He had no money to buy the books which he would love to read. Whenever he would come to know about someone who had a good book to read, he would go and read the book there. Once he came to know that on the other part of the river there was a retired judge who had a great collection of law books. Lincoln at that time wanted to visit the retired judge so that he could read the books. But the point was it was a time when the winter season was on. The river was with ice water but still Lincoln took the small boat and proceeded to the residence of the former justice across the river. Half way he crossed the river but his boat got struck with an ice rock on the river and the boat got broken. But still Lincoln did not accept the defeat. He challenged the defeat and crossed the river by swimming. After searching the residence of the judge he went and met the retired judge and requested the Honourable judge to show him some of the books. At that point of time the domestic servant of the judge was on leave and the judge was facing great difficulty in managing his own affairs. The judge agreed to give permission to Lincoln to read the books provided he was ready to work as a domestic servant at his residence. Lincoln accepted the condition of the former judge. Whole of the day he would work as a domestic servant at the residence of the judge, bring the wood from the jungle, do all domestic household work and at night sit down with the books to read them. The retired judge was very much impressed with the determination skill of Lincoln and ultimately he presented him many books out of love and affection. This is the actual story of Abraham Lincoln who became later on the President of USA only because of the power of determination. You too can achieve miracles in the world but only when you adopt to the power of determination.

102

Make your money work harder

A super successful person tries to avail, tries to explain others in every part of life activity one of the important activities of the life which enables a person to be super successful specially in the monetary world relates to making your money work harder. If one is to accept this theme as a part of one of the important activities of attaining super success, then definitely instead of keeping the money idle in your cupboard, you would start keeping the money in a bank savings account and thereafter switch over to taking advantage of en-cashing a bond better money option available to you in managing your money matter. It would be worthwhile to park the money in a liquid fund or park the money in short term fund or invest the money in fixed income instruments or finally invest a portion of the money in equity but every time your aim and motto is how to make money work harder. It is true to make money however difficult but important point is to retain the money and multiply the money much harder and this is the most important area on which the super successful person should always devote time and energy.

103

Get ready to prepare the balance sheet of your life

End of the day the health of a business enterprise is to be seen by the balance sheet of the organization. Similarly is the success and particularly the super success of a person is to be evaluated from the balance sheet of his life. Hence, prepare quarterly, half yearly and finally yearly balance sheet of your life. In this balance sheet the following details would act as a guide to you in preparing your balance sheet of life :-

Our birth is our opening balance.
Our death is our closing balance
Prejudiced views are our liabilities.
Our creative ideas are our asset.
Soul is our fixed asset.
Heart is our current asset.
Brain is our fixed deposit.
Thoughts are our current account.
Achievements are our capital.
Character and moral are our stock-in-trade.
Friends are our general reserves.
Values and behaviour are our goodwill.
Patience is our interest earned.
Love is our dividend.
Children are our bonus issues.
Education is brands/patents.
Knowledge is our investment.
Expenses are our premium account.
Our aim is to tally the balance sheet accurately.
.... And now you start preparation of your Balance Sheet.

104

Ready to read, read to grasp and grasp to implement

The super successful person should always find out time to read and read and read. Big question is what to read and the final answer is read something which inspires you. Read something that is away from your requirement of business or profession. Read something new and innovative which is not read by others and once you read, try to grasp the important points of what you have read and finally after grasping the important pointers by reading the books etc. now is the time to implement what you have read. I recollect what Francis Bacon, one of the greatest philosophers of the 15th Century wrote that 'Reading makes a full man, conference a ready man and writing an exact man'. Thus, first of all make yourself as a full man and make yourself as a super successful person to start eveloping the habit of reading and finally conclude the end result of reading by grasping the subject matter and by grasping something new and innovative and ultimately what you have read and grasp that to implement the same for achieving your super success.

105

Focus concentration of mind at every point in life

Mind is most important. The fact also remains that we hardly use 10 per cent of our mind in achieving success and prosperity. A super successful person in fact is able to use 15 per cent of his mind and still he has seen super success in life. But if you want to achieve something more than super success, or at least super success, then you should aim at focusing the concentration of mind at all point of time in life. Every time whenever you feel your mind should speak it should speak with complete concentration at your command. Do remember that concentration is possible by training your mind. The question is how to train the mind and the answer is simple that is meditation and meditation. Sit down in a calm cool place preferably at fixed point of time and just meditate 10 minutes and increase your intake of meditation by 10 minutes every week and let a stage come when you can meditate without any problem up to 60 minutes at a stretch. Once you meditate, then you are able to develop the power of concentration of mind. Do also remember that it is your concentration of mind which is responsible in making of the super successful person in you. I am very much impressed by the contents of Katha Upanishad which states that "He who is possessed of supreme knowledge by concentration of mind, must have his senses under control, like spirited steeds controlled by charioteer".

106

Make each day of life a joyous day

Happiness unlimited, should be the aim of your life. Only when you find happiness unlimited in your heart and around you, then you are surely entitled to give yourself the credit of being a super successful person. Merely having money, merely having fame and fame alone does not make you a super successful person. It is the holistic personality of yours which alone makes you a super successful person. Hence, every super successful person should make attempt to see that his life is a basket of joyous day today and tomorrow and every day thereafter. We are all part and parcel of the life's drama where sometimes we are the directors, sometimes the producers, sometimes the production man and sometimes the cameraman. However, what remains to be seen is that in every role which we play in life we must obtain and we must have happiness unlimited. It is worthwhile and simple interesting idea developed by me in the form of preparing your own happiness diary. Every day before you retire just take out 5 minutes from your schedule and write down on a piece of paper the pointers which provided happiness to you today and the pointers which provided you unhappiness to you today. Once you write down the diary of the day with reference to happiness, then yourself you give mark to today's day. Supposing you achieve good number of marks, then definitely you had wonderful day. If not, it is time for you to think of what next to do to make each day of life a joyous life. Also do remember only when you are able to have a joyful life, a happy life, then you find that the great illnesses which confronts us would be away from us. No dreadful disease like cancer etc. would never come near you. Also do remember that cancers etc. are a result of unhappiness and it affects very badly our consciousness and hence the body cell gets damaged. Therefore, it is time now that we aim every day to live a joyous life and to have unlimited happiness within us. Ageing would be a thing of past if you are happy every day.

107

Keep rudeness away

Erit Hoffer said that rudeness is the weak man's limitation of stress. My friend's mother Savita Sharma feels that rude and discourteous people. rude and discourteous people may get short-term results. Most people like to avoid dealing with such behavior and in the long run, rude people are disliked. Many people have destroyed their own success because they lack courtesy and manners. Courtesy is another name for politeness. It costs a little but pays a lot not only to the individual but also to the entire organization. Courteous behavior ought to be taught to children at an early age. So that they can grow and become mature considerate adults.

One should therefore, avoid always rudeness. If you are rude but still you are super successful person, then it is this quality of your rudeness that will make you from a super successful person to a successful person and finally this rudeness will take away the success in you and will take you to the non-successful arena in life. Hence, at every point of time in life always keep rudeness away.

108

Stop judging people merely by their appearance

A super successful person would always ensure that he would never judge a person just by his appearance alone. I remember a very true story by Nelcolm Forbes. This story will bring definitely a turning point in the minds of all those persons who would like to be super successful persons. This story by Nelcolm Forbes which was printed in Aryan Heritage is reproduced below with the aim that it would help providing a food for thought for all those who aspire to be super successful persons in life: A lady in a faded gingham dress and her husband , dressed in homespun threadbare suit, stepped off the train in Boston, and walked timidly without an appointment into the Harvard University President's outer office. The secretary could tell in moment that such backwoods; country hicks had no business at Harvard and probably didn't even deserve to be in Cambridge. "We'd like to see the president" the man said softly. : "He'll be busy all day" the secretary replied. "We'll wait" the lady replied. For hours the secretary ignored them, hoping that the couple would finally get discouraged and go away. They didn't , and the secretary grew frustrated and finally decided to disturb the president, even though it was a chore she always regretted. May be if you see them for a few minutes, they'll leave," she said to him! He sighed in exasperation and nodded. Someone of his importance obviously didn't have the time to spend with them, and he detested gingham dresses and homespun suits cluttering up his outer office. The president, stern faced, strutted toward the couple. The lady told him, "We had a son who attended Harvard for one year. He loved Harvard. He was happy here. But about a year ago, he was accidentally killed. My husband and I would like to erect a memorial to him, somewhere on campus. The president wasn't touched. He was shocked. "Madam", he said gruffly, "We can't put up a statue for every person who attended Harvard and died. If we did, this place would look like a cemetery." "Oh no! the lady explained quickly. "We don't want to erect a statue. We thought we would like to give a building to Harvard." The president rolled his eyes. He glanced at the gingham dress and homespun suit and then exclaimed, "A building! Do you have any earthly idea how much a building costs ? We have over seven and a half million dollars in the physical buildings here at Harvard." For a moment the lady was silent. The president was pleased. May be he could get rid of them now. The lady turned to her husband and said quietly, "Is that all it costs to start a university? Why don't we just start our own? Her husband nodded. The president's face wilted in confusion and bewilderment. Mr. and Mrs. Leland Stanford got up and walked away, traveling to Palo Alto, California, where they established the university that bears their name, Stanford University– a memorial to a son that Harvard no longer cared about.

Thus, if you are in the habit of judging people by their appearances, do amend this habit of yours and start believing on the dictum – never to judge persons with their appearance.

NEW BOOKS FROM THE
HOUSE OF DIAMOND
Dr. K.C. Mahendru
Baba Ramdev
Resurgence of New India......295.00
Dr. Kapil Kakkar
Secrets of Success
through BhagwadGeeta......95.00
Sri Sri Ravishankar
Walking The Path......179.00
Rajiv Tiwari
Commonwealth Games
2010......95.00
Rajiv Tiwari
Delhi : A Travel
Guide......125.00
Ashok Jain
Unlock the Door
to Success......125.00
Seema Seth
When Rahul Met Sunshine......95.00
Soumyashri Debashish
Love, Pride Paradox & Prophecy......95.00
Narendra Kohli
The Opportunity......150.00
(Ram Katha)
POSITIVE THINKING
IS SECRET OF SUCCESS
Matchless Creation of Biswaroop Roy Chowdhury
The 4th IDIOT
FREE VCD
ANCHOR - OMI VAIDYA
The Famous Charatcter of 3 Idiots Movie
Chatur Ramalingam
Anshu Pathak
Rainbow in Dew Drops......100.00
Rajee H. Singhania
Love in a Time Machine......95.00
Aabid Surti
Sufi......150.00
Prem Chand Sahajwala
Mumbai Kiski......100.00
Joginder Singh
Nothing is Impossible......150.00
Ashokindu
Power to Write
your own Destination......125.00
Biswaroop Roy Chowdhury
India Book of Records
2010......195.00
Dr. Sunil Vaid
Learn to slap your child......150.00
Ranu Saran
Choose Your Career......95.00
Davinder Singh Minhas
Tips & Trcks
Windows-7......150.00
Davinder Singh Minhas
Tips & Trcks
Excel-2010......150.00
Davinder Singh Minhas
Tips & Trcks
Word-2010......150.00
DIAMOND BOOKS
X-30, Okhla Industrial Area, Phase-II New Delhi-110020
Tel : 91+11-40712100, 40716600 Fax : 011-41611866 email : sales@dpb.in www.dpb.in

COMPUTER BOOKS

DYNAMIC MEMORY COMPUTER COURSE

Biswaroop Roy Chowdhury

In today's cyber world, not knowing about computer is nothing less than illiteracy. Knowing about computer and its uses is no more a luxury but a necessity. This book has been brought out keeping this necessity in mind. In this book the fantastic story of the computer from its inception to its vital state on covered. Every nuance from hardware to software, interest to networking & from MS-Office to Window XP/Vista, a reader will get all he wants to know about computers. Computer will be as clear as your drinking water.

Rs. 250.00

Dynamic Memory Windows Vista & Office 2007

Devender Singh Minhas

The technology of Windows and internet to computer system has created an open run way for new introductions. In this field as well, every new version overrides old version and comes forward with yet more power & features. *Window Vista* is one such latest version & this book updates its readers, with the novality. Devender Minhas has once again done his wonderful job.

Rs. 200.00

Dynamic Memory Windows 98/XP & Internet

Devender Singh Minhas

In the hi-tech world, not knowing about the computer is nothing less than illiteracy. Computer has become an intergral part of our life. Computer touches our every aspect of life making it easier and comfortable. So, knowing about computer and its uses are no more a knowledge but a necessity. This book has been brought forth keeping this necessity in mind. **Rs. 110.00**

Dynamic Memory Internet & E-mail

Davinder Singh Minhas

In today's educated world, not knowing about Internet is nothing less than illiteracy. This book will be a handy tool to become an expert on Internet. Every step from the equipments you need to have an Internet to the method of approaching an Internet Service provider. From E-mail to Internet safety and from Web browser to e-commerce, a reader will get all in this book. **Rs. 110.00**

Dynamic Memory Internet Dictionary

Tarun Chakarborty

This Internet Dictionary contains almost all the necessary Internet Terminology. Surely, it will benefit all those who are NET savvy and willing to know more about the endless world of WorldWide Web (WWW). **Rs. 110.00**

Dynamic Memory Computer Dictionary

Tarun Chakarborty

This dictionary is an essential guide to modern computer terminology and jargon and contains hundreds of straightforward definitions, example sentences and usage tips. The terms are illustrated wherever possible for the convenience of the readers.

Rs. 110.00

Books can be requisitioned by V.P.P. Postage charges will be Rs. 20/- per book. For orders of three books the postage will be free.

FUSION BOOKS X-30, Okhla Industrial Area, Phase-II, New Delhi-110020, Phone : 41611861 Fax : 41611866
E-mail : sales@dpb.in Website : www.dpb.in